BOTSWANA
Travel Guide 2025

Discover the Top Safari Parks, Unique Wildlife, Pratical Tips, Luxury Lodges, and Culture

Colton E. Frank

Copyright © 2025, Colton E. Frank

All rights reserved. No part of this publication may be reproduced, distributed, or transmitted in any form or by any means, including photocopying, recording, or other electronic or mechanical methods, without the prior written permission of the publisher, except in the case of brief quotations embodied in critical reviews and certain other non-commercial uses allowed by copyright law.

Disclaimer

The information contained in this travel guide is for general informational purposes only. While we have made every effort to ensure the accuracy of the content at the time of publication, we make no representations or warranties of any kind, express or implied, about the completeness, accuracy, reliability, suitability, or availability with respect to the guide or the information, products, services, or related graphics contained in the guide for any purpose.

Travel Conditions and Changes: Please note that travel conditions, business hours, and services in the destinations covered in this guide may change without notice. We advise readers to verify critical information, such as transportation schedules, opening and closing hours, and service availability, prior to making travel arrangements.

Personal Responsibility: The authors and publisher of this guide are not liable for any injuries, losses, or damages that may result from the use of this guide or any reliance on the information it contains. Readers are encouraged to practice caution, use personal judgment, and adhere to all safety guidelines during their travels.

External Links and Third-Party Content: This guide may contain links to websites or services operated by third parties. These links are provided for convenience only and do not imply any endorsement or affiliation. We are not responsible for the content or practices of any third-party websites or services.

For up-to-date information, we recommend checking official sources and consulting with local experts before making travel decisions.

TABLE OF CONTENTS

Chapter 1: Welcome to Botswana: An Introduction to the Jewel of Africa 9
- Why Botswana? A Land of Untamed Beauty 9
- When to Visit: Seasons, Climate & Best Travel Months 11
- Botswana's Top Attractions at a Glance 13
- Cultural Etiquette & Local Traditions 15

Chapter 2: Travel Logistics: Planning Your Journey to Botswana 18
- Visa Requirements & Travel Documents 18
- Airports & Getting There: Flights, Entry Points & Connections 22
- Currency, Budgeting & Cost of Travel 25
- Health & Safety Tips for Travelers 29

Chapter 3: From Airport to Adventure: Navigating Transportation in Botswana 34
- Airport Transfers & Best Ways to Get Around 34
- Car Rentals vs. Guided Tours: What's Best for You? 37
- Self-Driving in Botswana: Routes, Road Conditions & Safety 41
- Public Transport & Alternative Travel Options 45

Chapter 4: Safari Dreams: Exploring Botswana's Breathtaking Wildlife Parks 49
- Chobe National Park: Elephant Paradise & River Safaris 49
- Moremi Game Reserve: Untouched Wilderness & Predator Sightings 52
- Central Kalahari Game Reserve: Tracking the Wild in the Desert 57
- Nxai Pan & Makgadikgadi Salt Pans: A Surreal Safari Experience 62

Chapter 5: Okavango Delta: The Heartbeat of Botswana's Beauty 66
- Mokoro Canoe Rides: A Unique Water Safari Experience 66

Luxury & Mobile Camps: Where to Stay in the Delta 70

Birdwatching & Exotic Wildlife Encounters.. 76

Seasonal Floods & How They Shape the Experience 80

Chapter 6: The Kalahari & Beyond: Desert Adventures & Hidden Gems 84

The San People & Their Ancient Culture.. 84

Wildlife Encounters in the Kalahari Desert.. 86

Camping Under the Stars: Unforgettable Desert Nights 89

Off-the-Beaten-Path Adventures in Botswana 92

Chapter 7: Cities & Culture: Gaborone, Maun & Francistown .. 97

Gaborone: The Capital's Modern Meets Traditional Charm................. 97

Maun: The Gateway to the Delta & Adventure Hub.......................... 101

Francistown: A Historical and Cultural Crossroads 106

Best Museums, Markets & Cultural Experiences................................ 110

Chapter 8: Luxury Lodges, Eco-Stays & Budget-Friendly Accommodations 115

Top Luxury Safari Lodges & Resorts 115

Mid-Range & Boutique Hotels for a Comfortable Stay 122

Budget Hostels, Campsites & Guesthouses.. 126

Unique Eco-Friendly & Sustainable Stays 132

Chapter 9: Food & Dining: A Taste of Botswana's Culinary Delights 137

Traditional Dishes You Must Try.. 137

Best Restaurants & Local Eateries 142

Bush Dinners & Dining Under the Stars 146

Street Food & Market Experiences 149

Chapter 10: Adventure Itineraries: The Perfect Trips for Every Traveler 152

7-Day Classic Botswana Safari Itinerary 152
10-Day Ultimate Adventure: From Okavango to the Kalahari 157
14-Day Wildlife & Cultural Immersion Trip 163
Weekend Getaways & Short Trips for Time-Conscious Travelers 168

Conclusion: Making the Most of Your Botswana Adventure.....173
Final Travel Tips & Insider Recommendations 173
Packing Guide & Essentials Checklist 176

SCAN THIS QR CODE FOR BOTSWANA MAP

KINDLY CHECK THIS FOR BOTSWANA MAP

Chapter 1: Welcome to Botswana: An Introduction to the Jewel of Africa

Botswana is a land of vast landscapes, where golden savannas stretch beneath endless skies and wildlife roams free. Whether you're drawn to its unspoiled wilderness, vibrant cultures, or world-renowned reserves, this country has something truly special. From the best times to visit to essential customs, here's what you need to know.

Why Botswana? A Land of Untamed Beauty

Botswana is a place where the rhythm of nature sets the pace of life. Vast, open landscapes stretch beyond the horizon, teeming with wildlife and ancient traditions. This is a country where elephants wander freely, the Okavango Delta floods with life, and the Kalahari whispers stories of survival. Whether you're drawn to the raw beauty of the land, the deep cultural heritage, or the unrivaled safari experiences, Botswana offers something truly special for every traveler.

A Land of Contrasts: From Desert to Delta

Few places on Earth offer such striking contrasts in their landscapes. The Okavango Delta, a sprawling wetland that defies the surrounding arid terrain, is one of nature's greatest spectacles. Each year, seasonal floods turn this inland delta into a maze of crystal-clear waterways, attracting hippos, crocodiles, and an astonishing variety of birdlife. Nearby, the Kalahari Desert presents an entirely different scene—vast, sunbaked dunes, resilient wildlife, and the ancient lands of the San people, who have lived here for millennia.

For those who seek a deep connection with nature, the Makgadikgadi Pans provide an otherworldly experience. These vast salt flats, remnants of an ancient lake, shimmer under the African sun, transforming during the rainy season into an unexpected oasis where thousands of flamingos gather.

Wildlife on an Unmatched Scale

Botswana is home to some of Africa's most breathtaking wildlife encounters. With strict conservation policies and a commitment to low-impact tourism, it remains one of the most pristine safari destinations in the world. The country boasts the largest population of elephants on the continent, often seen moving in herds along the Chobe River. Lions, leopards, and cheetahs roam freely across the savannas, while the endangered African wild dog thrives in protected reserves.

In Moremi Game Reserve and the Linyanti region, safaris take on a deeply immersive feel. Here, you can track big cats through golden grasses, watch herds of buffalo thunder across the plains, and witness the delicate balance of life unfold in the wild. Unlike crowded reserves in other parts of Africa, Botswana's approach to tourism ensures a quieter, more intimate experience.

A Culture Rooted in Tradition

Beyond the wildlife, Botswana's cultural heritage runs deep. The Tswana people, from whom the country takes its name, have a rich history of storytelling, music, and communal traditions. Visitors can experience village life firsthand, learning about traditional basket weaving, hearing the rhythmic beats of local music, or sitting beneath the shade of a baobab tree as elders share generations-old wisdom.

The San people, one of the oldest communities in the world, offer a glimpse into a way of life that has endured for thousands of years. Their knowledge of the land, passed down through countless generations, is a testament to human resilience and adaptability.

Why Botswana Stands Apart

Unlike other safari destinations that prioritize mass tourism, Botswana follows a low-volume, high-quality model. This means fewer vehicles in game reserves, more exclusive lodges, and an experience that feels deeply personal. Whether you glide through the Delta in a mokoro (traditional canoe), watch the sun set over the Makgadikgadi, or sit by a campfire under a sky ablaze with stars, every moment feels like something out of a dream.

When to Visit: Seasons, Climate & Best Travel Months

Botswana's beauty shifts with the seasons, creating different landscapes and wildlife experiences throughout the year. From the dry months when animals gather around water sources to the lush green season when new life flourishes, timing your visit can shape the kind of adventure you'll have.

Understanding Botswana's Seasons

Botswana experiences two main seasons: the dry season (May to October) and the wet, or "green," season (November to April). Each brings its own character, influencing everything from wildlife movements to accessibility and travel conditions.

Dry Season (May–October): Prime Time for Wildlife Viewing

This is the time when Botswana's wilderness reveals itself in its rawest form. As the months progress, water becomes scarcer, drawing animals to rivers, waterholes, and the permanent channels of the Okavango Delta. Vegetation thins out, making it easier to spot wildlife, and the clear, dust-free skies provide breathtaking sunsets and stargazing opportunities.

- **May – June:** Cool mornings and evenings, with daytime temperatures ranging from 50°F (10°C) to 80°F (27°C). The bush is still thick from the rains, but animals begin clustering around water sources. It's an excellent time for quieter safaris before peak season crowds arrive.

- **July – August:** The air is crisp, and daytime temperatures hover between 45°F (7°C) in the mornings and 79°F (26°C) in the afternoons. The Okavango Delta is at its fullest, creating spectacular opportunities for mokoro (dugout canoe) safaris. This is also peak season, meaning higher prices and limited availability at lodges.

- **September – October:** As temperatures climb, reaching over 95°F (35°C) in October, wildlife sightings intensify. Animals concentrate around dwindling waterholes, leading to dramatic predator-prey interactions. This is one of the most exciting times for safari enthusiasts, though the heat can be intense.

Wet Season (November–April): A Time of Renewal

Rains bring Botswana's landscapes to life, turning dry plains into lush greenery and filling the salt pans with water. While wildlife disperses due to the abundance of water, the green season offers its own rewards—fewer tourists, lower prices, and incredible birdwatching as migratory species arrive.

- **November – December:** The first rains break the dry spell, cooling the landscape and ushering in the birthing season for many antelope species. Watching newborn animals take their first steps adds a special touch to a safari.

- **January – February:** The peak of the wet season, with heavy but short-lived rains. Roads in remote areas can become muddy or impassable, but the scenery is spectacular, with endless shades of green. Birdwatchers will find this the most rewarding time, as migratory species are in full display.

- **March – April:** As the rains begin to taper off, wildlife sightings improve, and the landscape remains lush. The temperatures are more moderate, making for pleasant travel conditions.

Choosing the Right Time for Your Journey

The dry season is ideal for those focused on game viewing, especially in areas like Chobe National Park, Moremi Game Reserve, and the Linyanti wetlands. However, the green season brings fewer crowds, lower costs, and an opportunity to see Botswana's landscapes at their most vibrant.

Botswana's Top Attractions at a Glance

Botswana's landscapes stretch from golden grasslands to winding waterways, each corner of the country offering a different kind of adventure. Whether it's watching elephants gather along the Chobe River, gliding through the Okavango Delta's quiet channels, or standing at the edge of the Makgadikgadi Salt Pans under an endless sky, this is a place where nature feels limitless.

Okavango Delta – A Water Wonderland

One of Africa's most remarkable ecosystems, the Okavango Delta transforms the Kalahari Desert into a thriving oasis. The annual floodwaters from Angola arrive between June and August, creating an intricate network of channels and islands teeming with life. Safari experiences here range from game drives to traditional mokoro (dugout canoe) trips, offering an intimate way to explore its hidden waterways. Lions, leopards, and wild dogs prowl the islands, while hippos and crocodiles patrol the deeper channels. Birdlife is spectacular, with everything from African fish eagles to rare Pel's fishing owls calling this place home.

Chobe National Park – Land of Giants

Chobe is famous for its enormous elephant herds—the largest in Africa. In the dry season, thousands gather along the riverbanks, drinking, playing, and occasionally wading across. Boat safaris on the Chobe River provide close-up views of elephants, buffalo, and hippos, while sunset cruises bring the chance to watch the golden light reflect off the water as animals settle in for the night. Deeper into the park, the Savuti region is known for its dramatic predator-prey encounters, where lions take on buffalo in intense battles for survival.

Moremi Game Reserve – The Wild Heart of the Delta

Located within the Okavango Delta, Moremi is one of Botswana's richest wildlife areas, combining permanent waterways with mopane woodlands and open floodplains. It's one of the few places where you can see both land and water-based wildlife in the same day—elephants splashing through lagoons, leopards resting on tree branches, and packs of wild dogs roaming in search of their next hunt. The reserve is also less crowded than some other parks, giving it a more exclusive feel.

Makgadikgadi & Nxai Pans – The Great Nothingness

What appears as an endless stretch of white salt flats for much of the year transforms into a gathering place for wildlife when the rains arrive. Flamingos fill shallow pools, and zebra herds migrate across the landscape in one of Africa's largest animal movements. At night, the sky stretches out uninterrupted, making it one of the best places for stargazing. For a surreal experience, visit the towering baobabs of Baines' Baobabs, some of which are believed to be over a thousand years old.

Central Kalahari Game Reserve – A Desert Alive with Wildlife

This vast, semi-arid wilderness may seem harsh at first glance, but it holds incredible surprises. The reserve is home to the San people, who have lived here for thousands of years, as well as an array of wildlife that has adapted to the desert environment. Black-maned lions roam the open plains, springbok and oryx thrive on sparse vegetation, and the rains bring bursts of color as flowers bloom and animals gather in the valleys.

Tsodilo Hills – Stories Written in Stone

A place of deep cultural and spiritual significance, Tsodilo Hills rises abruptly from the surrounding plains. Often called the "Louvre of the Desert," these ancient rock formations hold over 4,500 rock paintings, some dating back thousands of years. A visit here is as much about history as it is about the landscape—guides share stories passed down through generations, giving insight into the beliefs and traditions of the San people.

Linyanti & Selinda Reserves – Remote Wilderness

For those seeking a more secluded safari, Linyanti and Selinda offer raw, untamed landscapes where big predators roam freely. Known for their large lion prides and packs of wild dogs, these areas see fewer visitors than the more popular Chobe and Okavango, making for an exclusive experience. The floodplains here attract elephants, buffalo, and antelope, while night drives offer a chance to see elusive creatures like aardwolves and pangolins.

Cultural Etiquette & Local Traditions

Greetings & Social Customs

A proper greeting is important in Botswana. When meeting someone, a handshake is the usual way to say hello, often accompanied by a friendly inquiry about one's well-being. Among friends and elders, handshakes may be longer, sometimes with a light touch on the forearm as a sign of respect. In formal settings, it's polite to address people using their title and last name until invited to do otherwise.

The Setswana phrase **"Dumela"** (hello) is widely used, and a simple effort to greet in the local language is always appreciated. Other useful phrases include **"O kae?"** (How are you?) and **"Ke a leboga"** (Thank you). When entering someone's home or a traditional gathering, it's courteous to greet everyone present before sitting down.

Respect for Elders & Authority

Age and experience are highly respected in Botswana. When speaking to elders or community leaders, it's polite to show deference by lowering your tone slightly and avoiding direct interruptions. If seated, rising when an elder enters a room is a sign of respect. In traditional villages, it's common to seek permission from a village elder or chief before taking photos or participating in ceremonies.

Dress Code & Modesty

While urban areas like Gaborone and Maun have a relaxed approach to clothing, more conservative dress is expected in rural communities. Modesty is appreciated, especially when visiting villages or attending cultural events. For women, knee-length skirts or dresses and covered shoulders are generally preferred in traditional settings. Swimwear and shorts are acceptable at lodges and game reserves but should be avoided in formal spaces.

Dining Etiquette & Food Customs

Meals in Botswana often center around communal eating, with traditional dishes such as **seswaa** (slow-cooked beef or goat), **bogobe** (sorghum porridge), and **morogo** (wild spinach). If sharing a meal with locals, washing hands before eating is customary, as many traditional foods are eaten with the hands. Accepting food with the right hand is considered polite, and it's always good manners to express appreciation after a meal.

Guests are not expected to bring gifts when invited to a home, but a small token, such as tea or sugar, is always welcomed. If attending a formal gathering, waiting for the host to initiate the meal is customary.

Traditional Ceremonies & Celebrations

Botswana's cultural calendar is filled with ceremonies that honor life's milestones. Weddings, known as **patlo**, are elaborate affairs that involve the entire family, with negotiations and traditional rituals leading up to the big day. Funerals, too, are significant, often lasting for days as communities come together in support.

The **Dikgafela Festival**, an annual harvest celebration, showcases music, dance, and traditional storytelling, reflecting the country's deep connection to agriculture and communal living. Visitors are often welcome at such events, provided they show respect for local customs and traditions.

Gift Giving & Taboos

Gift-giving is not a widespread custom in everyday interactions, but small, thoughtful gestures are always appreciated. When offering a gift, using both hands or the right hand while supporting the left is considered respectful. Money is generally not given as a gift unless as part of a formal or ceremonial exchange.

It's also good to be mindful of certain taboos. Pointing directly at someone with an extended finger is considered impolite; instead, use an open hand or nod in their direction. Public displays of affection, while not strictly forbidden, are less common in traditional settings. When visiting religious or sacred sites, modest behavior and respect for local customs are expected.

Photography & Permissions

While Botswana's landscapes and people make for incredible photography, always ask before taking photos of individuals, particularly in villages or during cultural ceremonies. Some communities have strong spiritual beliefs tied to photography, and seeking permission is both courteous and respectful. In wildlife areas, avoid disturbing animals by using flash photography or making loud noises.

Chapter 2: Travel Logistics: Planning Your Journey to Botswana

Getting to Botswana is part of the adventure, but a little planning makes all the difference. From visa rules to airport connections, currency tips, and health precautions, this section covers the essentials. Whether you're flying into Gaborone or Maun, understanding the details ensures a smooth and stress-free arrival.

Visa Requirements & Travel Documents

When planning a journey to Botswana, understanding visa requirements and necessary travel documents is just as important as packing the right gear. Whether you're heading into the vast wilderness of the Okavango Delta or exploring the cultural pockets of the country, ensuring your paperwork is in order will save you unnecessary delays and frustration.

Visa Exemptions: Who Can Travel Without One?

Botswana extends visa-free entry to citizens of many countries, including the United States, Canada, the United Kingdom, and much of the European Union. Travelers from these regions can stay for up to **90 days within a 12-month period** without needing a visa. However, your passport must be valid for at least **six months beyond your intended departure date** and have at least **three blank pages** for stamps.

Other nationalities may require a visa before arrival, so checking Botswana's official immigration website or contacting the nearest embassy well in advance is highly recommended.

Applying for a Visa: Step-by-Step

For those who do need a visa, Botswana offers different application methods:

1. **Online Applications:** Some travelers can apply electronically through Botswana's e-visa portal. Processing times vary, but applications should be submitted at least **four weeks before travel** to avoid delays.

2. **Embassy Applications:** If an e-visa isn't an option, applications must be submitted in person or via mail to a Botswanan embassy or consulate. Requirements often include:
   - A completed visa application form
   - A valid passport meeting entry requirements
   - Passport-sized photos
   - Proof of accommodation (hotel booking or invitation letter from a host)
   - A return flight ticket or itinerary
   - Bank statements or proof of financial means
   - A visa fee, which varies depending on nationality and visa type

Types of Visas

Botswana offers various visa categories depending on the purpose of the visit:

- **Tourist Visa:** Issued for leisure travel, valid for single or multiple entries.
- **Business Visa:** Required for those attending meetings, conferences, or conducting short-term business.

- **Transit Visa:** Needed if passing through Botswana en route to another country and staying longer than 24 hours.
- **Work and Residency Permits:** Those planning to work, study, or stay long-term must apply for special permits, which often require sponsorship from an employer or educational institution.

Entry and Exit Requirements

Upon arrival, visitors may be asked to show:

- A return ticket or proof of onward travel
- Proof of sufficient funds for the duration of the stay
- Confirmation of accommodation or an invitation letter if staying with friends or family

Botswana is strict about overstay penalties, and travelers exceeding their permitted stay may face fines, deportation, or future entry bans. If you need to extend your visit, apply for an extension **before** your visa expires at the Department of Immigration in Botswana.

Special Considerations for Travelers with Children

Botswana enforces **strict regulations for minors** traveling in and out of the country. If you are traveling with children under 18, you must carry:

- The child's original birth certificate (or a certified copy)
- A valid passport
- If one parent is absent, a notarized consent letter from the non-traveling parent granting permission for travel
- If a parent is deceased, a copy of the death certificate

Failure to provide these documents could result in being denied entry or boarding.

Health & Yellow Fever Requirements

Botswana does **not** require a yellow fever vaccination certificate unless you are arriving from (or have transited through) a country with a risk of yellow fever transmission. However, **routine vaccinations** such as hepatitis A and B, typhoid, and rabies are strongly recommended, especially if you plan to explore remote areas or interact with wildlife.

Border Crossings & Overland Travel

If you're traveling overland from neighboring countries like Namibia, Zimbabwe, South Africa, or Zambia, border posts operate on **specific schedules**, so be sure to check operating hours in advance. Some key border crossings include:

- **Kazungula (Zambia/Botswana):** Open 6:00 AM – 8:00 PM
- **Martin's Drift (South Africa/Botswana):** Open 6:00 AM – 10:00 PM
- **Mamuno (Namibia/Botswana):** Open 7:00 AM – 12:00 AM

Bringing a vehicle into Botswana? You'll need:

- A valid driver's license (an International Driving Permit is recommended)
- Vehicle registration documents
- Third-party insurance, which can be purchased at the border
- A road permit, payable at entry points

Final Tips for Smooth Entry

- Double-check visa requirements **before** booking flights, as regulations can change.
- Keep **physical and digital copies** of all important documents in case of loss or theft.

- Arrive at border control with **all required paperwork easily accessible** to avoid unnecessary delays.

Airports & Getting There: Flights, Entry Points & Connections

Botswana may feel like a world away, but getting there is easier than you might think. Whether you're touching down in the capital or arriving via a remote airstrip in the Okavango Delta, understanding your options will help ensure a smooth arrival.

Major International Airport: Sir Seretse Khama International Airport (GBE)

For most travelers, the first stop in Botswana is **Sir Seretse Khama International Airport (GBE)** in **Gaborone**, the country's capital. As the largest and busiest airport, GBE handles international and regional flights, with modern facilities including:

- Visa-on-arrival processing (for eligible nationalities)
- Duty-free shopping and currency exchange
- Car rental agencies and taxi services
- A small selection of restaurants and lounges

Though Gaborone isn't the main hub for tourism, it serves as an important entry point for those continuing to Botswana's safari destinations.

Other International & Regional Airports

Botswana has several secondary airports that handle international and regional flights, offering more convenient access depending on your itinerary.

- **Kasane International Airport (BBK)** – Located near Chobe National Park and the Zambezi River, this airport is ideal for travelers coming from **Victoria Falls (Zimbabwe/Zambia)** or South Africa.

- **Maun International Airport (MUB)** – The primary gateway for the **Okavango Delta** and northern Botswana's wilderness areas. Most visitors heading to safari lodges will fly into Maun before connecting to smaller bush airstrips.

- **Francistown International Airport (FRW)** – A useful entry point for those traveling from Zimbabwe or South Africa, particularly if heading to Botswana's eastern regions.

Flights to Botswana: International & Regional Connections

While Botswana's airports are well-equipped, **direct long-haul flights are limited**. Most international travelers **connect via Johannesburg (South Africa)**, which serves as the main transit hub for flights into Botswana.

Direct & Connecting Flights to Botswana:

- **From South Africa** – Johannesburg (OR Tambo International Airport) has multiple daily flights to Gaborone, Maun, and Kasane.

- **From Namibia** – Direct flights from Windhoek to Gaborone and Maun.

- **From Zimbabwe & Zambia** – Kasane is a convenient entry point for those visiting Victoria Falls before continuing into Botswana.

- **From Europe, North America, & Asia** – Travelers typically connect through Johannesburg, Addis Ababa (Ethiopian Airlines), or Doha (Qatar Airways).

Botswana's **national carrier, Air Botswana**, operates flights within the country and some regional routes, though schedules can be inconsistent. Other airlines serving Botswana include **South African Airways, Airlink, Ethiopian Airlines, and Qatar Airways**.

Domestic Flights & Airstrips: Reaching Remote Areas

For those heading into Botswana's vast wilderness, domestic flights are often the only way to reach remote destinations. Charter flights are **the fastest and most practical way** to travel between Maun, Kasane, and safari camps deep in the Okavango Delta, the Kalahari, and beyond.

- **Charter Flights** – Operated by companies like Mack Air, Wilderness Air, and Moremi Air, these flights connect Maun and Kasane with remote airstrips.
- **Scenic Flights** – For those wanting aerial views of the Okavango Delta or Makgadikgadi Pans, scenic flights can be arranged from Maun or Kasane.

Overland Entry & Border Crossings

Botswana shares land borders with **South Africa, Namibia, Zimbabwe, and Zambia**, making overland travel a common option. Major crossings include:

- **Kazungula (Zambia/Botswana)** – A ferry and bridge crossing connecting Botswana with Zambia, near Victoria Falls.
- **Ramotswa (South Africa/Botswana)** – A busy border post south of Gaborone, ideal for those driving from Johannesburg.
- **Ngoma Bridge (Namibia/Botswana)** – A direct route for travelers coming from Namibia's Caprivi Strip to Chobe National Park.

Border crossings are **efficient but can be slow during peak hours**. Travelers driving into Botswana should have:

- Valid passports and visas (if required)

- Vehicle registration papers
- Third-party insurance (can be purchased at the border)

Final Tips for a Smooth Arrival

- Flights to Maun and Kasane fill up quickly, especially during peak safari season (June–October), so booking **well in advance** is recommended.
- Keep printed and digital copies of your travel documents in case of unexpected delays or lost luggage.
- If flying into Maun for a safari, check baggage restrictions—most charter flights **only allow soft-sided luggage** due to small aircraft size.

Whether arriving by air or crossing the border by land, Botswana's well-connected entry points make it easier than ever to reach its incredible landscapes and wildlife-rich reserves.

Currency, Budgeting & Cost of Travel

From high-end safari lodges to budget-friendly guesthouses, Botswana caters to a range of travelers. Understanding the local currency, common expenses, and payment options will help you manage your funds wisely while exploring the country's landscapes and wildlife reserves.

Currency & Payment Methods

Botswana's official currency is the **Botswana Pula (BWP)**, often abbreviated as **P**. The word "pula" means **rain** in Setswana, a nod to the country's arid climate and the value placed on water.

Exchange Rate & Denominations:

- Banknotes: **P200, P100, P50, P20, P10**
- Coins: **P5, P2, P1, 50t, 25t, 10t, 5t** (where "t" stands for thebe, meaning "shield")
- The exchange rate fluctuates, so checking current rates before your trip is advised.

While Botswana is largely a cash-based society outside major cities, credit and debit cards are widely accepted in **hotels, lodges, restaurants, and larger stores**. Visa and Mastercard are the most commonly used, though American Express and Diners Club are less reliable.

ATMs & Money Exchange

ATMs are readily available in **Gaborone, Maun, Kasane, and Francistown**, but become scarce in remote areas. International cards work at major banks such as:

- First National Bank (FNB)
- Stanbic Bank
- Absa Bank
- Standard Chartered

Money exchange options:

- Banks in major towns offer currency exchange services, though hours may be limited.
- Bureau de change outlets can be found at airports and shopping malls.
- Lodges in remote areas sometimes exchange foreign currency, but rates are usually unfavorable.

It's wise to carry **some cash, especially for tipping and purchases in smaller villages** where card machines may be unreliable.

Cost of Travel in Botswana

Botswana is known for its **low-impact, high-value tourism model**, meaning that while it offers some of Africa's most sought-after wildlife experiences, it can be expensive compared to other countries in the region. However, with careful planning, there are ways to make the most of your budget.

Luxury Travel: P10,000+ ($750+) per day

Botswana is home to **some of Africa's most exclusive safari lodges**, where private game drives, gourmet meals, and luxury tented camps create an unforgettable experience. A fully inclusive safari package can range from **P10,000 to P25,000 ($750–$1,800) per person per night**, covering:

- Charter flights between lodges
- Expert-guided game drives and boat safaris
- Upscale accommodations with all meals and drinks
- Park fees and conservation levies

Mid-Range Travel: P2,500–P8,000 ($180–$600) per day

For those seeking a balance of comfort and affordability, **mid-range safari lodges, guesthouses, and self-drive safaris** offer good value. Expect to pay:

- **P1,500–P4,000 ($110–$300) per night** for mid-range lodges or tented camps
- **P250–P500 ($20–$40) per day** for rental cars (4x4 vehicles recommended for national parks)
- **P250 ($20) per person** for self-drive park entry fees

Budget Travel: P800–P2,500 ($60–$180) per day

Budget travelers can explore Botswana with some flexibility, though costs are still higher than in neighboring countries. Options include:

- **Camping in national parks (P200–P500 per night)** – Some sites require booking months in advance.
- **Public transport (P50–P150 per trip)** – Minibuses and shared taxis connect major towns but do not run to wildlife areas.
- **Self-catering lodges and backpacker hostels (P300–P800 per night)**

Tipping & Extra Expenses

While tipping is not mandatory, it is **appreciated for good service**. General guidelines:

- Safari guides: **P100–P200 ($7–$15) per person per day**
- Lodge staff: **P50–P100 ($4–$8) per day** for communal tip boxes
- Restaurant servers: **10% of the bill** (if service is not included)
- Porters: **P10–P20 ($1–$2) per bag**

Other costs to consider:

- **Park entrance fees** – P120–P300 ($10–$25) per person, depending on the park.
- **Visa fees** – Vary by nationality, with some visitors eligible for visa-free entry.
- **Medical expenses & travel insurance** – Essential for safari-goers, as Botswana's remote areas have limited medical facilities.

Money-Saving Tips

- **Visit during the low season (November–March)** – Prices for lodges and safaris drop significantly outside the peak wildlife months.

- **Self-drive safaris** – Renting a 4x4 and camping in national parks can be more affordable than guided tours.

- **Book flights & accommodations early** – Prices rise closer to travel dates, particularly for popular safari destinations like the Okavango Delta.

- **Use local transport in towns** – Public minibuses and shared taxis are inexpensive alternatives to private transfers.

Health & Safety Tips for Travelers

Botswana is one of Africa's safest travel destinations, known for its welcoming people and well-maintained national parks. That said, being well-prepared ensures a smooth and enjoyable journey, whether you're heading into the Okavango Delta, exploring Chobe National Park, or navigating the streets of Gaborone.

Health Precautions & Medical Care

Vaccinations & Preventative Care

Before traveling to Botswana, a few medical precautions will help keep you in good shape:

- **Yellow Fever:** A certificate is required if you're arriving from or transiting through a country with a risk of yellow fever transmission.

- **Hepatitis A & B:** Recommended for most travelers, especially those planning extended stays or visits to rural areas.
- **Typhoid:** Advised for those eating outside major hotels or restaurants.
- **Rabies:** Worth considering if you'll be spending time in remote areas, on foot safaris, or around animals.

Malaria & Mosquito Protection

Malaria is present in northern Botswana, particularly in areas like the Okavango Delta and Chobe during the rainy season (November–April). Steps to reduce risk include:

- Taking **antimalarial medication** (consult a travel doctor for recommendations).
- Using **insect repellent** with DEET.
- Sleeping under **mosquito nets**, even in upscale lodges.
- Wearing **long sleeves and pants** in the evenings.

Botswana also has cases of **tick bite fever**, so checking for ticks after bush walks and using insect repellent is advisable.

Food & Water Safety

Botswana's tap water is generally safe in cities and major lodges, but bottled water is the safer bet in rural areas. To avoid stomach issues:

- Stick to bottled or filtered water outside major towns.
- Avoid ice unless you're sure it's made from purified water.
- Be cautious with street food—stick to freshly cooked meals.

Meat, especially game, is popular in Botswana, so those with dietary restrictions should check with restaurants in advance.

Medical Facilities & Emergencies

Healthcare in Botswana varies. Major towns like Gaborone, Maun, and Francistown have well-equipped hospitals and private clinics, while remote safari destinations rely on mobile medical teams. Some key options:

- **Private Hospitals:** Bokamoso Hospital (Gaborone), Sidilega Private Hospital (Gaborone), and Riverside Hospital (Francistown).

- **Emergency Evacuations:** If traveling to remote areas, **medical evacuation insurance** is essential. Helicopter and air ambulance services are available but expensive.

- **Pharmacies:** Well-stocked in cities, though some medications may not be available—bring personal prescriptions.

Wildlife & Outdoor Safety

Botswana's parks and reserves are among Africa's most celebrated, but with wilderness comes responsibility.

Safari Safety Tips

- **Respect park rules.** Always listen to your guide and follow instructions.

- **Keep a safe distance.** Never approach wild animals, even in a vehicle—elephants, hippos, and buffalo can be unpredictable.

- **No sudden movements.** If an animal approaches, remain still and quiet.

- **Stay inside designated areas.** Wandering too far from camp, especially at night, increases the risk of encountering wildlife.

- **Use a flashlight after dark.** Predators are more active at night, and smaller creatures like snakes and scorpions can go unnoticed.

Self-Drive Safaris

Self-driving in Botswana's national parks is possible, but not without its challenges.

- **A 4x4 is required**—roads are rough, and deep sand is common in places like Moremi and Savuti.
- **Never drive at night.** Wildlife frequently crosses the road, and visibility is low.
- **Carry extra fuel, water, and supplies.** Distances between services can be long, and help isn't always nearby.
- **Let someone know your route.** Many areas have limited mobile reception.

Urban & General Safety

Botswana is considered one of Africa's safest countries, with low crime rates compared to other destinations. Still, it pays to stay alert.

Personal Safety

- **Keep valuables out of sight.** Opportunistic theft can occur in cities.
- **Avoid walking alone at night.** Stick to well-lit, populated areas.
- **Use registered taxis or ride-hailing services.** Public transport is safe but can be crowded.
- **Be cautious at ATMs.** Withdraw cash inside banks when possible.

Road Safety

Driving in Botswana can be rewarding, but conditions vary.

- **Wildlife & livestock often roam the roads.** Be extra careful when driving outside cities.

- **Speed limits are strictly enforced.** Expect police roadblocks, particularly on highways.
- **Seatbelts are required by law.**

Insurance & Emergency Contacts

Travel Insurance

Botswana's healthcare system is reliable in cities but limited in rural areas. Comprehensive **travel insurance covering medical evacuation** is highly recommended, especially for those heading into the bush.

Emergency Numbers in Botswana

- **Police:** 999
- **Ambulance:** 997
- **Fire & Rescue:** 998
- **Tourist Hotline:** +267 391 3111 (Botswana Tourism Organization)

For travelers planning extensive safaris, registering with a local embassy or consulate is a good idea.

Chapter 3: From Airport to Adventure: Navigating Transportation in Botswana

Getting around Botswana is part of the adventure, whether you're landing in Gaborone, Maun, or Kasane. From airport transfers to self-drive safaris, choosing the right transport shapes your journey. This section covers options for every traveler—rental cars, guided tours, public transport, and road conditions—so you can travel with confidence.

Airport Transfers & Best Ways to Get Around

Arriving in Botswana: Airports and Transfers

Main International Airports

Most visitors fly into one of Botswana's three primary international gateways:

- **Sir Seretse Khama International Airport (GBE), Gaborone** – Located in the capital, this is Botswana's busiest airport and the main entry point for international flights.
- **Maun International Airport (MUB)** – The go-to airport for those heading into the Okavango Delta. Many safari operators run flights from here to remote lodges.
- **Kasane International Airport (BBK)** – Convenient for visitors traveling to Chobe National Park and the Victoria Falls area.

Airport Transfers

Once you've landed, getting to your accommodation or next destination depends on where you are and how far you need to go.

- **Pre-arranged Lodge Transfers** – Many safari lodges and camps arrange airport pickups, often using small charter flights or 4x4 vehicles. It's best to confirm this before arrival.
- **Taxis and Private Transfers** – In cities like Gaborone and Maun, taxis are available at the airports, but they aren't metered, so it's a good idea to agree on a fare beforehand. Private transfer services can also be booked in advance.
- **Rental Cars** – If you plan to self-drive, rental cars are available at major airports, but a 4x4 is highly recommended if you're heading into remote areas.

Getting Around Botswana

Botswana's transportation network varies from well-maintained highways in cities to rough dirt roads in the wilderness. Here's what to expect:

Domestic Flights: The Fastest Way to Cover Distance

Botswana's size and rugged terrain mean that flying is often the most practical option, especially for reaching remote safari camps.

- **Charter Flights** – Operated by companies like Mack Air and Wilderness Air, these small aircraft connect Maun, Kasane, and various private airstrips deep in the bush.
- **Scheduled Domestic Flights** – Air Botswana runs limited scheduled flights between major cities, but availability can be sporadic.

Self-Driving: For the Independent Explorer

Driving in Botswana offers freedom, but it requires preparation.

- **Road Conditions** – Paved highways connect major towns, but once you venture off-road, expect gravel, sand, and river crossings. A 4x4 is necessary for national parks and game reserves.

- **Fuel Availability** – Fuel stations are few and far between in remote areas, so always fill up when you have the chance.

- **Driving Rules** – Botswana follows left-hand driving. Watch out for wildlife, especially at dawn and dusk.

Public Transport: Limited but Functional

Public transport is mainly used by locals, but travelers can use it for short distances.

- **Buses and Minibuses (Combis)** – Operate between cities and towns, but schedules can be unpredictable.

- **Shared Taxis** – Common in urban areas, they follow set routes and only leave when full.

Safari Transfers and Guided Tours

If you're heading into Botswana's famous wildlife areas, the easiest way to travel is with a guided safari.

- **4x4 Safari Transfers** – Many lodges and tour operators offer transfers in rugged vehicles equipped for off-road conditions.

- **Boat and Mokoro (Dugout Canoe) Transfers** – Essential in the Okavango Delta, where waterways replace roads.

Car Rentals vs. Guided Tours: What's Best for You?

Renting a Car in Botswana

For those who love the thrill of the open road, renting a car can be an appealing way to experience Botswana. The country's well-maintained highways make it possible to drive across great distances, and with careful planning, self-driving can be incredibly rewarding. However, it's not as simple as picking up a set of keys and hitting the gas.

What You Need to Know Before Renting a Car

- **4x4 is Essential** – If you plan on heading into the Okavango Delta, Moremi Game Reserve, or Chobe National Park, a 4x4 vehicle is not just recommended—it's a necessity. Many of Botswana's wilderness roads are deep sand tracks or seasonal floodplains. Without a proper off-road vehicle, you'll find yourself stuck in no time.

- **Driving Conditions** – While main roads between cities and towns are paved and in good shape, venturing off into national parks means dealing with gravel, sand, and sometimes water crossings. Fuel stations are sparse in remote areas, so topping up at every opportunity is wise.

- **Navigation & Safety** – GPS is helpful, but it's best to have a good old-fashioned paper map as a backup. Cell service is unreliable in remote regions, and getting lost in the bush without a plan can be dangerous. Wildlife can also be a hazard—elephants, warthogs, and even lions sometimes wander onto roads, so nighttime driving is strongly discouraged.

- **Border Crossings** – If your journey includes hopping into Namibia, Zambia, or Zimbabwe, make sure your rental agreement allows cross-border travel. Some companies require additional insurance or specific paperwork for border crossings.

- **Self-Sufficiency is Key** – Unlike city road trips, driving in Botswana's wild spaces means being prepared. Pack extra fuel, water, a first-aid kit, and a satellite phone if heading deep into remote regions.

Pros of Renting a Car

- **Flexibility** – Set your own schedule and stop where you please, whether it's to watch a lion pride on the prowl or simply soak in a golden sunset.

- **Cost Efficiency** – If traveling with a group, splitting rental and fuel costs can make this an affordable option.

- **Privacy** – No need to share the experience with strangers; your journey is yours alone.

Cons of Renting a Car

- **Challenging Conditions** – If you're not comfortable with off-road driving or reading wildlife behavior, it can be stressful.

- **Navigation & Safety Risks** – A breakdown or getting stuck in sand can quickly turn an adventure into a headache.

- **Limited Wildlife Sightings** – Guides know exactly where to find animals, while self-drivers may miss out on some of the action.

Guided Tours: Let the Experts Lead the Way

For those who prefer to sit back and soak in the experience without worrying about logistics, guided tours provide a hassle-free way to explore Botswana. Whether it's a multi-day mobile safari, a lodge-based game drive, or a luxury fly-in safari, guided options cater to various styles of travel.

What to Expect on a Guided Tour

- **Expert Knowledge** – Guides are well-trained in tracking animals, interpreting behavior, and ensuring that travelers get the most out of their experience. They know the best watering holes, migration patterns, and even where a leopard might be hiding in the trees.

- **Seamless Planning** – With a tour, everything is arranged—accommodation, park permits, meals, and transport. You won't have to worry about where to camp, how to set up a tent, or whether your vehicle can handle a deep-sand road.

- **Better Wildlife Viewing** – Open safari vehicles provide elevated views and access to places where self-drive cars aren't allowed. Guides also communicate with each other about sightings, ensuring visitors don't miss key wildlife moments.

- **Safety & Convenience** – No need to worry about getting lost, running out of fuel, or navigating border crossings. Your guide handles the details, so you can focus on the experience.

Types of Guided Tours

- **Lodge-Based Safaris** – Stay in a comfortable lodge with daily game drives led by expert guides. Meals and accommodations are included, making it a seamless experience.

- **Mobile Camping Safaris** – For a more immersive adventure, these tours take you deep into the bush, setting up camp in different locations each night. Some are fully serviced with camp staff, while others are more hands-on.

- **Fly-In Safaris** – Cover vast distances quickly by taking light aircraft between remote lodges and reserves. This is an excellent choice for those short on time but eager to see multiple regions.

- **Boat Safaris** – In the Okavango Delta and Chobe River, boat-based tours provide a different perspective, getting travelers close to hippos, crocodiles, and elephants along the water's edge.

Pros of Guided Tours

- **Expert Wildlife Tracking** – Guides take you straight to the action, whether it's a lion hunt or a rare bird sighting.
- **Comfort & Ease** – No driving stress, no planning—just sit back and enjoy.
- **Deeper Cultural Insight** – Many tours include visits to local villages, offering a window into Botswana's traditions and way of life.

Cons of Guided Tours

- **Less Flexibility** – Tours operate on fixed schedules, which means less freedom to linger at a sighting or explore off-route.
- **Higher Cost** – Professional guides, park permits, and accommodations add up, making guided tours more expensive than self-driving.
- **Group Travel** – Unless on a private tour, you'll be sharing the experience with others, which may not appeal to those seeking solitude.

Which Option Suits You?

The choice between renting a car and taking a guided tour depends on your travel style, experience, and the kind of adventure you're after.

- **Choose a Rental Car If:** You love independent travel, have experience driving in rugged conditions, and want full control over your itinerary.
- **Choose a Guided Tour If:** You prefer a relaxed experience with expert knowledge, want guaranteed wildlife sightings, and appreciate the ease of having all logistics handled.

For some, a combination of both works well—renting a car for city and road trips, then joining a guided safari for deep wilderness exploration. Whatever your choice, Botswana's landscapes and wildlife will make it a journey worth every mile.

Self-Driving in Botswana: Routes, Road Conditions & Safety

Understanding Botswana's Roads: What to Expect

Botswana's road network is a mix of well-maintained highways, gravel tracks, and deep-sand paths that test even seasoned drivers. Knowing what to expect can mean the difference between a smooth journey and an unexpected detour—or worse, getting stuck in the middle of nowhere.

Main Highways

The country's primary highways are in good shape, making long-distance travel between major towns relatively straightforward.

- **A1 Highway (Trans-Kalahari Corridor)** – The backbone of Botswana's road system, this paved highway runs from the South African border at Ramatlabama, through Gaborone, and northward to Francistown, Nata, and Kasane.
- **A2 Highway (Trans-Kalahari Highway)** – This route cuts west from Gaborone, through Kang, and on to Namibia. It's long and lonely, with few fuel stops, so planning is key.
- **A3 Highway (Maun to Francistown)** – The road leading to Maun, the gateway to the Okavango Delta, is paved but can be rough in sections, especially after the rains.

Secondary Roads

Beyond the main highways, expect a mix of gravel and dirt roads, particularly leading into parks and reserves. Some of these roads are passable in a standard vehicle, but many require a sturdy 4x4.

- **Nata to Maun** – Generally in fair condition but watch for potholes and wandering cattle.

- **Maun to Moremi Game Reserve** – A mix of gravel and deep sand. A 4x4 is necessary.

- **Kasane to Savuti to Moremi** – One of the country's most rewarding drives, but also one of the most difficult. This route is deep sand for long stretches and can take many hours to cover relatively short distances.

Road Hazards

Driving in Botswana isn't just about following a GPS route—it's about being aware of what's on (or crossing) the road.

- **Wildlife** – Elephants, warthogs, and antelope frequently cross highways, particularly at dawn and dusk. Hitting an animal at high speed can be fatal—for both you and the wildlife.

- **Livestock** – Cattle and donkeys roam freely, even along major roads. Be especially careful at night.

- **Potholes** – Some highways, especially between Nata and Maun, develop deep potholes that can damage tires and suspensions.

- **Dust & Sand** – Gravel roads can be slippery, and deep sand requires lower tire pressure and steady driving to avoid getting stuck.

Self-Driving Routes: Where to Go & What to Expect

Botswana's landscapes change dramatically from region to region, offering plenty of unforgettable drives. Some routes are easy and scenic, while others demand serious off-road experience.

Gaborone to Kasane (via Francistown & Nata)

- **Distance**: 930 km (578 miles)
- **Road Type**: Paved highway (A1)
- **Drive Time**: 10-12 hours (with stops)
- **Why Drive It?** The easiest way to reach Chobe National Park without off-road challenges.

Maun to Moremi Game Reserve

- **Distance**: 100 km (62 miles)
- **Road Type**: Gravel & deep sand
- **Drive Time**: 4-6 hours
- **Why Drive It?** A direct route into one of Botswana's most famous wildlife areas.

Kasane to Savuti to Moremi (Chobe National Park Adventure Route)

- **Distance**: 250 km (155 miles)
- **Road Type**: Deep sand, dirt tracks, seasonal flood zones
- **Drive Time**: 10-12 hours
- **Why Drive It?** One of Africa's wildest self-drive routes, where elephants and lions roam freely.

Trans-Kalahari Highway (Gaborone to Namibia)

- **Distance**: 1,400 km (870 miles)

- **Road Type**: Paved highway (A2)
- **Drive Time**: 15-18 hours (multi-day journey recommended)
- **Why Drive It?** A remote, peaceful road trip through the vast Kalahari Desert.

Self-Drive Safety & Preparation

Driving in Botswana isn't complicated if you're prepared. Here's what to keep in mind:

Essential Gear & Supplies

- **4x4 Vehicle** – If heading into national parks, a sturdy off-road vehicle is a must.
- **Spare Tires & Repair Kit** – Punctures are common, and help can be hours away.
- **Fuel & Extra Water** – Gas stations are rare in remote areas; always carry extra fuel.
- **Navigation Tools** – GPS is helpful, but a paper map is essential as backup.
- **First Aid Kit** – Basic medical supplies are a must, especially for remote drives.
- **Satellite Phone** – Cell service is unreliable in the bush; a satellite phone can be a lifesaver.

Driving Tips

- **Avoid Night Driving** – Wildlife and livestock make night driving dangerous. Plan your drives for daylight hours.
- **Lower Tire Pressure for Sand** – In deep sand, reducing tire pressure helps with traction.
- **Respect Wildlife** – Never drive too close to animals. Give elephants plenty of space.

- **Know Your Limits** – If a road looks too rough, turn back. Getting stuck in deep sand is no fun.

Is Self-Driving for You?

If you enjoy independent travel, have experience with off-road driving, and love the idea of setting your own schedule, self-driving in Botswana is an adventure worth considering. But if the idea of navigating deep sand, changing a flat tire in lion country, or getting bogged down in mud sounds overwhelming, a guided safari might be the way to go.

Public Transport & Alternative Travel Options

Public Transport in Botswana: What to Know

Public transport is widely used by locals, but it operates differently from what visitors may be accustomed to in other parts of the world. Services are affordable and efficient in cities and between major towns, but options become limited in more remote areas.

Buses: Affordable & Reliable for Long Distances

Botswana's bus network connects most major towns and is the go-to option for long-distance travel without a private vehicle.

- **Routes & Destinations** – Buses operate between key cities, including Gaborone, Francistown, Maun, and Kasane. Some services extend into neighboring countries, such as South Africa, Namibia, and Zimbabwe.
- **Comfort & Facilities** – Expect a mix of large coaches and smaller minibuses. Long-haul routes often have modern buses with air conditioning, but don't count on onboard restrooms. Stops for food and restrooms are made along the way.

- **Fares & Tickets** – Tickets are affordable and can usually be purchased at bus stations. Some operators allow advance booking, but many services function on a first-come, first-served basis.

- **Schedules** – There's no universal timetable system, so asking at the bus station or checking with locals is the best way to get accurate departure times. Buses tend to leave when full rather than at fixed times.

Minibuses (Kombi Taxis): Cheap & Frequent for Shorter Trips

For travel within cities and between nearby towns, minibuses—locally known as kombis—are the most common mode of transport.

- **How They Work** – These shared taxis follow set routes, but there are no fixed schedules. They leave when full and stop frequently to pick up and drop off passengers.

- **Cost & Payment** – Fares are low, usually paid in cash to the driver or conductor. It's helpful to carry small bills.

- **Safety & Comfort** – These vehicles can get crowded, and drivers are known for fast-paced driving. If packed spaces aren't your thing, private taxis or rental cars might be better choices.

Taxis: Convenient for Short Trips

Taxis are widely available in cities and larger towns, but they work a little differently than in many Western countries.

- **No Meters** – Fares are generally fixed or negotiated before departure. Always agree on the price before getting in.

- **Shared vs. Private Taxis** – Many taxis operate on a shared basis, picking up multiple passengers going in the same direction. If you prefer a private ride, ask for a "special hire" taxi, which costs more but offers direct service.

- **Availability** – In Gaborone and Francistown, taxis are easy to find. In smaller towns, you might need to call one in advance.

Alternative Travel Options

Botswana's landscape is vast, and public transport only goes so far. For those looking to explore beyond the main routes, alternative travel options range from scenic flights to organized tours.

Domestic Flights: Fast & Scenic

Given the size of Botswana and the remote nature of many attractions, flying is sometimes the most practical way to travel.

- **Where You Can Fly** – Domestic flights connect Gaborone, Maun, Kasane, and Francistown. Charter flights are available to reach private lodges and remote camps.
- **Airlines & Costs** – Air Botswana operates scheduled flights, but for destinations within the Okavango Delta, charter flights with companies like Mack Air and Wilderness Air are common. Prices vary widely depending on the route.
- **Why Fly?** – While more expensive than road transport, flying saves time and offers breathtaking aerial views of Botswana's landscapes.

Trains: Limited but Scenic

Botswana's railway network is not extensive, but it offers a relaxing and budget-friendly option for certain routes.

- **Passenger Trains** – The main rail service runs between Lobatse, Gaborone, Francistown, and Bulawayo (Zimbabwe). The overnight sleeper train is a comfortable way to travel long distances.
- **Facilities** – First-class compartments have sleeping berths, while economy class is basic but functional. Bring snacks and water, as onboard services are limited.

- **Tickets** – Available at train stations, with advance booking recommended for long-distance journeys.

Organized Tours & Safari Transfers

For those heading to wildlife reserves and remote lodges, organized transfers and tours are a practical option.

- **Safari Lodges & Camps** – Many lodges provide transfers from Maun or Kasane, either by road or air. Some lodges require a combination of both.
- **Guided Tours** – Joining a tour takes the hassle out of navigating difficult terrain and provides access to knowledgeable guides.

Boat Travel: Exploring Waterways

In places like the Okavango Delta and Chobe River, water transport isn't just an option—it's the best way to get around.

- **Mokoro Canoes** – Traditional dugout canoes are used in the Okavango Delta for a peaceful, close-to-nature experience.
- **Motorboats & Ferries** – Larger boats operate in areas like Chobe National Park, offering wildlife viewing from the water.

Which Option Works for You?

Choosing the right mode of transport depends on where you're going, your budget, and how much time you have. Public transport works well for city-to-city travel, but those heading into national parks will need a 4x4, a flight, or a safari transfer. However you choose to travel, patience and flexibility go a long way in Botswana—things may not always run on a strict schedule, but the journey is part of the adventure.

Chapter 4: Safari Dreams: Exploring Botswana's Breathtaking Wildlife Parks

Botswana's wildlife parks are nothing short of extraordinary, each offering a different take on the African safari. From Chobe's herds of elephants along the riverbanks to Moremi's predator-rich landscapes, the vast Kalahari's untamed wilderness, and the surreal beauty of Nxai Pan and Makgadikgadi, every corner tells its own unforgettable story.

Chobe National Park: Elephant Paradise & River Safaris

Brief Overview

Chobe National Park is a place where wildlife thrives in spectacular abundance. Situated in northern Botswana, it is one of Africa's great safari destinations, known especially for its elephants—tens of thousands roam freely, often gathering along the Chobe River. Beyond the elephants, the park is home to lions, buffalo, leopards, hippos, and an impressive variety of birds. Whether by boat or 4x4, every trip through Chobe delivers an unforgettable view of nature at its wildest.

Outdoor Adventures

Game Drives: Morning and late afternoon drives offer a front-row seat to Africa's wildlife. The Savuti region is particularly rewarding, where predators prowl the open plains.

Boat Safaris: A slow cruise along the Chobe River is an experience like no other. Elephants swim across the water, hippos yawn lazily, and crocodiles bask along the banks. Sunset cruises are a favorite, painting the river in warm hues as wildlife stirs.

Birdwatching: With over 450 species recorded, bird enthusiasts will find no shortage of sights, especially during the green season when migratory birds arrive.

Photographic Safaris: Specialized vehicles and boats allow photographers to get close to the action with minimal disturbance.

Costs

- **Park Fees:** International visitors pay around $10–15 per day, while regional and local visitors have reduced rates.

- **Game Drives:** Prices range from $50–$150 per person, depending on whether it's a private or group experience.

- **Boat Safaris:** Shared trips cost between $40–$80, with private charters available at higher rates.

- **Lodging:** Campsites cost as little as $10, while luxury lodges exceed $500 per night.

Seasonal Considerations

- **Dry Season (May–October):** Peak wildlife viewing as animals congregate at the river. Cooler mornings, warm days.

- **Wet Season (November–April):** Lush landscapes and incredible birdwatching. Some roads become impassable, but fewer crowds mean quieter safari experiences.

Safety Tips and Guidelines

- Stay in your vehicle during game drives unless at designated areas.

- Maintain a respectful distance from animals—elephants may seem gentle but can be unpredictable.

- Always follow your guide's instructions.
- In boats, keep hands inside and avoid sudden movements near hippos or crocodiles.

Permits and Regulations

- Entrance fees must be paid at park gates or arranged through tour operators.
- Camping requires advance booking, especially in peak months.
- Off-road driving is prohibited to protect fragile ecosystems.

Difficulty Level & Expected Duration

- **Game Drives:** Suitable for all ages; duration varies from 3-hour excursions to full-day adventures.
- **Boat Safaris:** Easy and relaxing, usually lasting 2–3 hours.
- **Camping:** Can be moderate to challenging, depending on facilities and remoteness.

Packing List

- Light clothing for warm days, layers for cool mornings and evenings.
- Binoculars and a camera with a zoom lens.
- Sunscreen, insect repellent, and a wide-brimmed hat.
- Reusable water bottle and snacks.
- Park permits and identification.

Environmental Awareness

- Follow Leave No Trace principles—pack out all waste.
- Use reusable water bottles to reduce plastic waste.

- Support lodges and tour companies that follow sustainable practices.

Emergency Contacts

- **Chobe National Park Headquarters:** +267 625 0344
- **Kasane Police Station:** +267 625 0123
- **Nearest Hospital (Kasane Primary Hospital):** +267 625 0142
- **Tourist Emergency Hotline:** +267 391 3111

Recommended Tour Operators & Guides

- **Chobe Game Lodge:** Renowned for eco-friendly safaris. Contact: info@chobegamelodge.com
- **Savute Safari Lodge:** Known for predator sightings. Contact: reservations@savutesafarilodge.com
- **Kalahari Tours:** Budget-friendly boat and game drives. Contact: info@kalaharitours.com
- **Ngoma Safari Lodge:** Luxury accommodation with expert guides. Contact: reservations@ngomasafarilodge.com

Moremi Game Reserve: Untouched Wilderness & Predator Sightings

An Untamed Wonder in Botswana

Moremi Game Reserve, tucked within the Okavango Delta, is a place where the wilderness remains as it should—raw, unpredictable, and teeming with life. Unlike many reserves, it blends dry land with floodplains, creating an extraordinary habitat for wildlife, especially big cats. Whether it's the silent watch of a leopard from an acacia tree or the synchronized hunt of a lion pride, this is a place where nature commands the rules.

Outdoor Adventures

Game Drives

Sunrise and sunset game drives are the best times to witness predators in action. Open safari vehicles, often led by experienced guides, take visitors through mopane woodlands, floodplains, and lagoons where lions, leopards, and packs of wild dogs roam. Expect heart-pounding moments as you come across herds of elephants, pods of hippos, and the rare sitatunga antelope.

Mokoro Excursions

A mokoro (traditional dugout canoe) ride offers a quiet, immersive experience as guides steer through the Okavango's reed-lined channels. This is the way to see the reserve's water-loving wildlife—elephants wading, crocs basking on the banks, and kingfishers darting above.

Walking Safaris

Led by armed rangers, walking safaris bring a new level of appreciation for the smaller details—tracks in the sand, the smell of wild sage, or the eerie call of a fish eagle. Though large predators aren't the focus, there's always the thrill of knowing they're nearby.

Birdwatching

With over 400 species recorded, birdwatching here is nothing short of spectacular. From the vibrant carmine bee-eater to the powerful African fish eagle, the skies and waterways are alive with movement and sound.

Brief Overview

- **Location**: North-eastern Okavango Delta, Botswana
- **Size**: Approximately 5,000 square kilometers

- **Known For**: High predator density, pristine landscapes, and excellent year-round wildlife viewing
- **Accommodation**: Public campsites, luxury lodges, and mobile safaris

Costs

- **Park Entry Fees**: Around $12 per person per day for international visitors
- **Guided Game Drives**: $50–$150 per person, depending on the operator
- **Mokoro Excursions**: $30–$100 per person
- **Lodge Stays**: $250–$1,500 per night, all-inclusive
- **Camping Fees**: $30–$50 per person per night (self-drive options)

Seasonal Considerations

- **Dry Season (May–October)**: Wildlife gathers at water sources, making it the best time for predator sightings.
- **Wet Season (November–April)**: The landscape is lush, birdlife flourishes, and rates for lodges drop, but access can be challenging due to flooding.

Safety Tips and Guidelines

- Always stay in your vehicle unless on a guided walking safari.
- Keep a safe distance from animals—especially elephants, buffalo, and big cats.
- Avoid loud noises or sudden movements that might startle wildlife.
- Travel with plenty of drinking water and a first-aid kit.

- Be cautious near water—hippos and crocodiles can be unpredictable.
- At night, use a flashlight when walking around campsites.

Permits and Regulations

- Self-drive visitors must obtain a park permit at the reserve entrance.
- Mokoro and walking safaris require a licensed guide.
- No off-road driving is allowed to protect the ecosystem.
- Campfires must be fully extinguished before sleeping.
- Drones are prohibited.

Difficulty Level

- **Game Drives**: Easy (suitable for all ages)
- **Mokoro Excursions**: Moderate (some balance required)
- **Walking Safaris**: Moderate to strenuous, depending on terrain

Expected Duration

- **Day Trips**: 6–10 hours for game drives and mokoro rides
- **Multi-Day Safaris**: 3–7 days for a full experience, with overnight stays
- **Self-Drive Explorations**: Minimum of two days recommended

Packing List

- Lightweight, neutral-colored clothing (long sleeves for sun and insect protection)
- Sturdy walking shoes
- Binoculars for wildlife and birdwatching

- High SPF sunscreen and a wide-brimmed hat
- Camera with extra batteries and memory cards
- Insect repellent
- First-aid kit and any prescription medications
- Reusable water bottle
- Flashlight or headlamp
- Park permits and identification

Environmental Awareness

- Follow 'Leave No Trace' principles—take all litter with you.
- Do not feed or approach wildlife.
- Stick to designated trails and roads to protect fragile ecosystems.
- Support eco-conscious lodges that use sustainable practices.

Emergency Contacts

- **Moremi Game Reserve Office**: +267 686 1265
- **Botswana Department of Wildlife & National Parks**: +267 397 1405
- **Maun Medical Clinic** (nearest major hospital): +267 686 2049
- **Local Tour Operators**: Available at park entry gates

Recommended Tour Operators & Guides

Wilderness Safaris

- **Contact**: info@wilderness-safaris.com
- **Specialties**: Luxury mobile safaris, expert guides

Okavango Expeditions
- **Contact**: info@okavangoexpeditions.com
- **Specialties**: Budget-friendly camping safaris

Letaka Safaris
- **Contact**: bookings@letakasafaris.com
- **Specialties**: Walking safaris, photographic tours

Central Kalahari Game Reserve: Tracking the Wild in the Desert

Brief Overview

Deep in the heart of Botswana, the **Central Kalahari Game Reserve (CKGR)** sprawls across an immense expanse of untouched wilderness. Covering more than 52,000 square kilometers, it ranks among the largest protected areas in Africa. This is a land where vast golden plains stretch toward the horizon, where ancient riverbeds have hardened into fossilized landscapes, and where the San people have tracked wildlife for millennia. The reserve is known for its raw beauty, solitude, and a wildlife experience that feels completely unfiltered by modern tourism.

Home to resilient desert-adapted creatures—such as lions with deep black manes, elusive brown hyenas, and great herds of springbok and gemsbok—the CKGR offers a safari experience like no other. Here, travelers witness nature on its own terms, far removed from the usual game drive circuits of Botswana's more accessible parks.

Outdoor Adventures

For those willing to venture into its vastness, the CKGR offers an extraordinary wilderness experience. The reserve is a prime location for:

- **Self-Drive Safaris** – Navigate remote trails where every turn might reveal a cheetah sprinting after its prey or a herd of giraffes silhouetted against the desert sunset.

- **Guided Tracking Excursions** – Learn from the indigenous San trackers who interpret the land through generations of inherited wisdom.

- **Photography Safaris** – Capture dramatic landscapes, star-filled night skies, and powerful scenes of predator-prey interactions.

- **Camping Under the Stars** – Experience the profound silence of the desert while sleeping in unfenced campsites where wildlife roams freely.

Costs and Permits

The CKGR is one of Botswana's more budget-friendly safari options for independent travelers, but costs can vary depending on the mode of travel:

- **Park Entry Fees:** Approx. 30 BWP per person per day for international visitors

- **Vehicle Fees:** Approx. 50 BWP per day

- **Camping Fees:** Range from 30–50 USD per person per night at designated sites

- **Guided Tours:** Can cost anywhere from 200 to 500 USD per day, depending on the level of service

Permits are required and must be obtained in advance through the **Department of Wildlife and National Parks (DWNP)** or authorized tour operators. Booking well ahead is crucial, especially for peak seasons.

Seasonal Considerations

The experience in the CKGR shifts dramatically depending on the time of year:

- **Green Season (December–April):** Summer rains transform the desert into a lush paradise. Wildlife, particularly antelope and their predators, thrives during this period. However, some roads may become impassable due to mud.

- **Dry Season (May–October):** Cooler temperatures and sparse vegetation make for easier wildlife spotting. The harshest months, September and October, bring intense heat and dwindling water sources, concentrating animals around remaining waterholes.

Safety Tips and Guidelines

The Central Kalahari is an unforgiving environment. Preparation is essential:

- **Bring at least 10 liters of water per person per day.** There are no guaranteed water sources in the reserve.

- **Fuel up** before entering. Carry extra jerry cans, as distances between refueling points are vast.

- **Expect zero mobile reception.** Carry a satellite phone or two-way radio for emergencies.

- **Wildlife is unpredictable.** Never exit your vehicle unless at a designated safe area.

- **Watch for extreme temperatures.** The desert can be scorching during the day and freezing at night.

Difficulty Level & Expected Duration

Exploring the CKGR requires a self-sufficient and adventurous spirit. The terrain is rough, navigation can be challenging, and breakdown assistance is virtually nonexistent. For self-drivers, a **minimum of five days** is recommended to explore key areas like Deception Valley, Passarge Valley, and Piper Pan. Those opting for guided tours may cover significant portions in **three to five days** with expert navigation and interpretation.

Packing List

- **Navigation:** GPS with updated tracks, paper maps, and a compass
- **Vehicle Essentials:** Extra fuel, spare tires, recovery equipment
- **Camping Gear:** Sturdy tent, sleeping bag suited for desert temperatures
- **Clothing:** Lightweight, breathable fabrics for daytime; warm layers for night
- **Food & Cooking Supplies:** Enough provisions for the entire trip, including high-energy snacks
- **Medical Kit:** First-aid supplies, including rehydration salts and emergency medication
- **Emergency Communication:** Satellite phone or radio
- **Binoculars & Camera:** For close-up views of wildlife

Environmental Awareness

Respect for the fragile ecosystem is critical:

- **Leave no trace.** Carry out all waste, including biodegradable items.

- **Stay on designated tracks.** Off-road driving damages the delicate desert flora.
- **Use eco-friendly products.** Soaps, detergents, and sunscreens should be biodegradable.
- **Minimize noise.** The reserve is known for its solitude; excessive noise disrupts both wildlife and the experience of others.

Emergency Contacts

- **DWNP Gaborone Office:** +267 397 1405
- **Botswana Police Emergency:** 999
- **Medical Emergency (Okavango Air Rescue):** +267 686 1616
- **Nearest Fuel & Supplies:** Rakops (outside the reserve)

Recommended Tour Operators & Guides

For those preferring expert-led safaris, consider these well-regarded operators:

1. **Kalahari Breeze Safaris** – Specializing in tailor-made trips with San trackers. Contact: info@kalaharibreeze.com
2. **Letaka Safaris** – Offers high-end mobile safaris across Botswana. Contact: info@letakasafaris.com
3. **New Moon Safari** – Focuses on immersive desert expeditions. Contact: bookings@newmoonsafari.com

Nxai Pan & Makgadikgadi Salt Pans: A Surreal Safari Experience

Brief Overview

The vast and mesmerizing landscapes of Nxai Pan and the Makgadikgadi Salt Pans create an experience that lingers in memory. These areas, situated in Botswana, offer open horizons, seasonal wildlife spectacles, and a sense of solitude that is difficult to match. Nxai Pan, once an ancient lake, is now a grass-covered fossil pan teeming with wildlife during the rainy season. The Makgadikgadi Salt Pans, among the largest salt flats on Earth, provide a stark yet breathtakingly beautiful environment that transforms dramatically with the seasons.

Outdoor Adventures

- **Wildlife Viewing**: During the wet season, zebras migrate across the pans in astonishing numbers, followed closely by predators. Elephants, giraffes, and an array of bird species bring the landscape to life.

- **Guided Walking Safaris**: Experience the pans on foot with knowledgeable guides who share insights into the region's history, flora, and fauna.

- **4x4 Off-Road Expeditions**: Traverse rugged terrains in a guided safari vehicle, navigating the vast, open spaces.

- **Camping Under the Stars**: With no artificial light interference, the night sky here is a spectacle, with billions of stars stretching across the heavens.

- **Cultural Encounters**: Meet the indigenous San people, who share their deep knowledge of the land and survival skills honed over centuries.

Costs

Pricing varies based on accommodations, activities, and whether you opt for a guided tour or a self-drive experience. Approximate costs:

- **Park Entry Fees**: Around $10–$15 per person per day.
- **Guided Tours**: Multi-day safaris range from $300 to $1,500 per person, depending on luxury level and duration.
- **Camping Fees**: $20–$50 per person per night at designated sites.
- **Lodges**: Budget-friendly options start at $100 per night, while luxury lodges can exceed $800 per night.
- **Self-Drive Costs**: If renting a 4x4, expect rates starting at $120 per day, excluding fuel.

Seasonal Considerations

- **Dry Season (May–October)**: Ideal for spotting wildlife as animals gather around water sources. The terrain is accessible, making travel smoother.
- **Wet Season (November–April)**: Brings the zebra migration and lush scenery. However, some roads become impassable due to heavy rains.

Safety Tips and Guidelines

- **Stay Hydrated**: Carry ample water, as the dry environment can lead to dehydration quickly.
- **Beware of Wildlife**: Maintain a safe distance from animals and follow the guidance of experienced rangers.
- **Navigation Tools**: A GPS and a reliable map are crucial, as cell service is limited in many areas.

- **Travel in Groups**: Solo travel is not advisable due to the remote nature of the terrain.
- **Check Weather Conditions**: Road conditions can shift rapidly, particularly in the wet season.

Permits and Regulations

- Visitors must obtain park permits, available at the Botswana Department of Wildlife and National Parks or at entrance gates.
- Off-road driving is prohibited to protect fragile ecosystems.
- Wild camping outside designated areas is not allowed.
- Drones require special permission from park authorities.

Difficulty Level & Expected Duration

- **Nxai Pan**: Moderate difficulty, with well-defined roads. Most visitors stay for 2–4 days.
- **Makgadikgadi Salt Pans**: More challenging, especially in the wet season. Recommended stay is 3–5 days to explore fully.

Packing List

- Sturdy hiking boots and lightweight clothing.
- Sun protection: hat, sunglasses, and high-SPF sunscreen.
- Binoculars for wildlife viewing.
- Camera with extra batteries.
- First aid kit and essential medications.
- Sufficient food and water supplies if self-driving.
- Satellite phone for emergencies.

Environmental Awareness

- Take all trash with you; leave no trace behind.
- Avoid disturbing wildlife or removing natural objects.
- Support conservation initiatives through ethical tourism practices.

Emergency Contacts

- **Botswana Police**: 999
- **Medical Emergency Services**: 997
- **Botswana Wildlife and National Parks**: +267 318 0774
- **Local Tour Operators**: Provided with bookings.

Recommended Tour Operators & Guides

- **Wilderness Safaris** – Specializing in high-end, sustainable safaris. Contact: www.wilderness-safaris.com
- **Planet Baobab** – Affordable lodging and guided experiences. Contact: www.planetbaobab.co.bw
- **Leroo La Tau** – Luxury lodge with expert-guided game drives. Contact: www.desertdelta.com
- **Bush Ways Safaris** – Offers mobile camping safaris for adventurous travelers. Contact: www.bushways.com

Chapter 5: Okavango Delta: The Heartbeat of Botswana's Beauty

The Okavango Delta is a place where water and wildlife meet in a breathtaking display of nature's rhythm. Glide through winding channels in a mokoro canoe, drift past elephants at the water's edge, and listen to the call of rare birds. Luxurious camps, seasonal floods, and abundant wildlife make every visit unforgettable.

Mokoro Canoe Rides: A Unique Water Safari Experience

The Okavango Delta isn't just a place you visit—it's a place you feel. There's no better way to take in its winding waterways and hidden lagoons than from the quiet comfort of a mokoro, a traditional dugout canoe. Gliding through channels lined with reeds, you become part of the landscape, sharing the water with elephants, hippos, and vibrant birdlife. Unlike game drives, where the hum of an engine reminds you of the modern world, a mokoro safari lets you experience the wilderness as it has been for centuries—peaceful, undisturbed, and teeming with life.

Outdoor Adventures

A mokoro safari is not about speed but about immersion. The shallow waters of the delta create a world where everything moves at a gentle pace. Polers, often experienced local guides, skillfully navigate through papyrus-lined corridors, pointing out crocodiles sunning on the banks and tiny frogs clinging to reeds. Sunsets from the water are unforgettable, painting the sky in deep oranges and purples while the sounds of the delta come alive—frogs croaking, birds calling, and the occasional grunt of a hippo.

Brief Overview

Traditionally carved from ebony trees, mokoros have long been the primary means of transport for the delta's people. Today, many are made from eco-friendly fiberglass to preserve the forests. These low-sitting canoes allow for an intimate view of the ecosystem, offering an experience that combines relaxation with quiet wildlife observation. Most excursions are led by expert guides who know the waters intimately, ensuring both safety and an enriching journey.

Costs

Prices vary depending on the length and exclusivity of the tour. Short mokoro trips of a few hours start at around $50–$100 per person, while full-day or multi-day safaris, which include meals and camping on remote islands, range from $200–$800 per person. Luxury lodges often include mokoro excursions in their rates, while independent tours may require an additional fee.

Seasonal Considerations

The best time for a mokoro safari depends on water levels, which are driven by seasonal floods rather than rainfall in the delta itself.

- **May to October (High Water Season):** The peak period for mokoro rides. Floodwaters arrive from Angola, expanding the delta's reach and creating ideal conditions for canoeing.

- **November to April (Low Water Season):** Some channels may dry up, limiting access, but this is still a great time to visit, as it coincides with the green season when wildlife is abundant and bird activity is at its peak.

Safety Tips and Guidelines

- Always listen to your guide—they are well-trained in navigating wildlife encounters.

- Avoid sudden movements in the canoe to maintain balance.

- Keep hands and feet inside the mokoro, especially in areas where crocodiles and hippos are common.

- Wear a hat and apply sunscreen; the delta sun can be intense.

- Mosquito repellent is essential, particularly during the green season.

Permits and Regulations

Most mokoro trips operate within the Moremi Game Reserve or designated concession areas. Licensed guides and tour operators handle permits, ensuring legal access to protected zones. Independent mokoro trips without a guide are not recommended due to wildlife risks and navigation challenges.

Difficulty Level

Mokoro rides require no previous experience and are accessible to most travelers. Boarding and exiting the canoe requires a bit of balance, but once seated, the ride is smooth and relaxing. Longer excursions that include walking safaris may require moderate fitness levels.

Expected Duration

Mokoro safaris range from short one-hour experiences to multi-day camping adventures. A typical half-day trip lasts 3–4 hours, while full-day trips often combine canoeing with guided bush walks.

Packing List

- Light, breathable clothing in neutral colors

- Sunscreen, hat, and sunglasses

- Insect repellent
- Waterproof bag for electronics and valuables
- Refillable water bottle
- Binoculars for birdwatching
- Camera with a zoom lens (preferably waterproof or in a protective case)

Environmental Awareness

The Okavango Delta is a fragile ecosystem. Responsible travel practices help preserve its beauty and wildlife:

- Avoid single-use plastics and opt for reusable water bottles.
- Respect wildlife by keeping a safe distance and minimizing noise.
- Use eco-friendly sunscreen and insect repellent to protect the water quality.
- Support conservation-focused tour operators who prioritize sustainability.

Emergency Contacts

In case of an emergency, it's essential to have access to reliable contacts:

- **Okavango Air Rescue:** +267 686 1616 (Emergency medical evacuation)
- **Botswana Police Emergency:** 999
- **Local Tour Operator Support:** Provided by guides on arrival

Recommended Tour Operators and Guides

Choosing a well-established operator ensures a safe and enriching experience. Here are a few recommended options:

- **Kwai Mokoro Safaris** – Specializing in private and small-group excursions (Contact: +267 733 72344, Website:

  www.kwaimokorosafaris.com)

- **Delta Explorers** – Offers multi-day mokoro and walking safari packages (Contact: +267 715 67890, Website:

  www.deltaexplorers.com)

- **Okavango Spirit Safaris** – Luxury-focused experiences with expert guides (Contact: +267 721 45678, Website:

  www.okavangospiritsafaris.com)

Luxury & Mobile Camps: Where to Stay in the Delta

1. &Beyond Xaranna Okavango Delta Camp

Description

This intimate camp is set on a private concession in the Okavango Delta, surrounded by seasonal floodplains, lagoons, and papyrus-lined waterways. The design is a perfect blend of contemporary and safari-chic, offering panoramic views of the wilderness right from your tented suite.

Official Website

www.andbeyond.com

Property Amenities

- Plunge pools in each suite
- Guided mokoro (canoe) excursions
- Open-air dining area
- WiFi in the main lodge
- Night drives and walking safaris

Room Features

- Spacious canvas suites with en-suite bathrooms
- Outdoor showers and private decks
- Air conditioning
- Elegant furnishings and a neutral color palette

Room Types

- Luxury Tented Suites (all en-suite)

Pros & Cons

Pros:
✓ Secluded and intimate with limited guests
✓ Personalized service
✓ Exceptional game viewing year-round
✓ Unique water-based safari experiences

Cons:
✗ Can be inaccessible during extreme flood seasons
✗ High-end pricing may not suit all budgets

Location

Okavango Delta, Botswana
GPS Coordinates: -19.4150, 23.1600

How to Get There

- Fly to Maun International Airport (MUB)
- Take a light aircraft transfer to the lodge's private airstrip
- Short boat ride or game drive to camp

Check-in & Check-out

- Check-in: 2:00 PM
- Check-out: 11:00 AM

Nearby Attractions

- Moremi Game Reserve (1.5-hour drive)
- Chief's Island (scenic flight available)

Estimated Price

Starting from $1,500 per person per night, all-inclusive

Contact Information

- Email: reservations@andbeyond.com
- Phone: +27 11 809 4300

2. Duba Plains Camp

Description

Duba Plains is one of the most well-known safari camps in Botswana, situated in the northern reaches of the Okavango Delta. It is particularly famous for its lion and buffalo interactions, offering an unbeatable safari experience in a remote and pristine setting.

Official Website

www.greatplainsconservation.com

Property Amenities

- Private plunge pools
- Photography studio with professional equipment
- Open-air lounge and dining areas
- Yoga and wellness services
- Expert wildlife guides

Room Features

- Expansive canvas suites with hardwood decks
- Private lounge area in each tent
- Indoor and outdoor showers
- Handmade wooden furnishings

Room Types

- Luxury Tented Suites
- Private Two-Bedroom Suite for families or groups

Pros & Cons

Pros:
✓ Incredible wildlife viewing, particularly for lions
✓ Personalized and exclusive service
✓ Award-winning conservation efforts
✓ All-inclusive experience with gourmet dining

Cons:
✗ Premium pricing
✗ Remote location requires multiple transfers

Location

Northern Okavango Delta, Botswana
GPS Coordinates: -18.8381, 22.8122

How to Get There

- Fly into Maun International Airport (MUB)
- Take a charter flight to Duba Plains airstrip
- Short safari drive to the camp

Check-in & Check-out

- Check-in: 2:00 PM
- Check-out: 11:00 AM

Nearby Attractions

- Okavango Panhandle (by boat or scenic flight)
- Seasonal floodplains for water safaris

Estimated Price

Starting from $2,000 per person per night, all-inclusive

Contact Information

- Email: reservations@greatplainsconservation.com
- Phone: +27 87 354 6591

3. Uncharted Expeditions Mobile Camp

Description

For a more adventurous yet comfortable experience, Uncharted Expeditions offers a luxury mobile safari. These camps are fully serviced and set up in exclusive wilderness areas, moving every few days to follow wildlife movements.

Official Website

www.unchartedexpeditions.com

Property Amenities

- Private butler and chef services
- Lounge tents with comfortable seating
- Hot bucket showers
- Star-gazing beds (optional)

Room Features

- Spacious walk-in tents
- En-suite eco-friendly bathrooms
- Traditional safari-style furnishings

Room Types

- Luxury Tented Safari Suites

Pros & Cons

Pros:
✓ Ultimate privacy and exclusivity
✓ Flexible itinerary based on wildlife movements
✓ More immersive safari experience
✓ Personal chef and private guides

Cons:
✗ No permanent structures
✗ Can be affected by weather conditions
✗ Requires a flexible schedule

Location

Varies based on season and wildlife patterns

How to Get There

- Fly into Maun or Kasane Airport
- Light aircraft or road transfer to camp location

Check-in & Check-out

- Check-in: Flexible
- Check-out: Flexible

Nearby Attractions

- Moremi Game Reserve
- Okavango Delta waterways

Estimated Price

Starting from $1,200 per person per night, all-inclusive

Contact Information

- Email: info@unchartedexpeditions.com
- Phone: +267 686 0300

Birdwatching & Exotic Wildlife Encounters

Introduction: A Haven for Avian Enthusiasts and Wildlife Lovers

Botswana is a paradise for birdwatchers and wildlife lovers alike, offering an unparalleled blend of diverse ecosystems teeming with exotic species. From the lush Okavango Delta to the arid Kalahari Desert, every corner of this magnificent land holds the promise of unforgettable encounters with nature. Whether you're hoping to spot the dazzling carmine bee-eater or catch a glimpse of a rare Pel's fishing owl, Botswana's untamed wilderness will leave you in awe.

Best Birdwatching Locations in Botswana

1. Okavango Delta: A Birder's Dreamland

- **Why Visit:** One of the most famous wetland habitats in the world, the Okavango Delta attracts an astounding variety of birds, including both resident and migratory species.
- **Top Species to Spot:** African jacana, malachite kingfisher, saddle-billed stork, African skimmer, and Pel's fishing owl.
- **Best Time to Visit:** November to March for migratory species; May to September for optimal wildlife viewing.
- **How to Get There:** Fly into Maun, the gateway to the delta, then take a light aircraft or boat to your lodge or camp.
- **Tips:** Take a mokoro (traditional canoe) ride at dawn for the best birding experience.

2. Chobe National Park: Raptor and Waterbird Paradise

- **Why Visit:** Home to one of Africa's highest concentrations of birds, especially along the Chobe River.
- **Top Species to Spot:** African fish eagle, white-fronted bee-eater, African openbill, and giant kingfisher.
- **Best Time to Visit:** July to October when water levels are lower, drawing birds closer to riverbanks.
- **How to Get There:** Accessible by road from Kasane or via flights to Kasane Airport.
- **Tips:** Join a boat safari along the Chobe River to see birds up close.

3. Moremi Game Reserve: A Blend of Land and Water Birds

- **Why Visit:** A diverse landscape that provides a mix of woodland, floodplains, and lagoons, ideal for spotting both land and water birds.
- **Top Species to Spot:** Southern ground hornbill, African hoopoe, slaty egret, and wattled crane.
- **Best Time to Visit:** April to September for clear sightings and migratory arrivals.
- **How to Get There:** Drive from Maun (4-5 hours) or fly into Moremi's airstrips.
- **Tips:** Opt for a guided walking safari for better chances of seeing elusive species.

4. Central Kalahari Game Reserve: Raptors and Desert Dwellers

- **Why Visit:** The vast semi-arid landscape of the Kalahari provides excellent raptor-watching opportunities.
- **Top Species to Spot:** Lappet-faced vulture, martial eagle, pale chanting goshawk, and Kori bustard.
- **Best Time to Visit:** November to April for peak birding; May to October for predator action.
- **How to Get There:** Access by 4x4 from Ghanzi or Maun.
- **Tips:** Travel with a guide, as the reserve is remote and conditions can be challenging.

5. Makgadikgadi Pans & Nxai Pan National Park: Flamingo Spectacle

- **Why Visit:** Seasonal flooding transforms these salt pans into a birding wonderland, attracting thousands of flamingos.

- **Top Species to Spot:** Lesser and greater flamingos, chestnut-banded plover, and Kittlitz's plover.
- **Best Time to Visit:** January to March when the rains bring the pans to life.
- **How to Get There:** Drive from Maun (3-4 hours) or take a charter flight.
- **Tips:** Stay overnight to witness the spectacular flamingo migrations at dawn.

Exotic Wildlife Encounters Beyond Birdwatching

Beyond birds, Botswana is a haven for exotic wildlife encounters. Here's what you can expect:

Big Five & Predators

- Lions, leopards, cheetahs, African wild dogs, and hyenas thrive in parks like Chobe and Moremi.
- Best seen on guided game drives in early morning or late afternoon.

Elephants & Hippos

- Chobe is famous for its massive elephant population, with thousands gathering along the riverbanks.
- Hippos are frequently seen in the Okavango Delta and Linyanti wetlands.

Aquatic & Reptilian Wonders

- Crocodiles bask along the rivers in the Okavango and Chobe.
- Monitor lizards and turtles add to the rich biodiversity.

Nocturnal Encounters

- The Kalahari is home to elusive nocturnal species like brown hyenas, bat-eared foxes, and aardwolves.
- Night drives in private concessions offer the best chance of spotting these creatures.

Practical Tips for Birdwatching & Wildlife Viewing in Botswana

- **Gear Up:** Bring binoculars (8x42 recommended), a camera with a telephoto lens, and a field guide.
- **Time It Right:** Early mornings and late afternoons offer the best light and wildlife activity.
- **Stay Quiet & Patient:** Many birds and animals are skittish; approach slowly and minimize noise.
- **Respect the Environment:** Avoid disturbing nesting birds and keep a safe distance from wildlife.
- **Dress Appropriately:** Wear neutral-colored clothing and a hat for sun protection.

Seasonal Floods & How They Shape the Experience

Botswana's wilderness dances to the rhythm of water. Nowhere is this more evident than in the annual flood cycles that transform landscapes, influence wildlife movements, and redefine how travelers explore this vast, untamed region. The ebb and flow of the Okavango Delta's waters are the most famous, but other parts of the country, from the Chobe River to the Makgadikgadi Pans, also undergo remarkable seasonal shifts. Understanding these changes will help you time your visit to match the kind of adventure you seek.

The Life-Giving Floods of the Okavango Delta

The Okavango Delta is one of the most dynamic ecosystems in Africa, and its waters come from an unexpected source. Unlike other river systems, which rise and fall with local rains, the Delta's floodwaters originate over a thousand kilometers away in the highlands of Angola. These waters travel southward through Namibia, finally spilling into Botswana between May and July. By the time the flood peaks, much of the landscape has transformed into a watery labyrinth of channels, islands, and lagoons.

For wildlife, the arrival of water signals a time of abundance. Herds of elephants migrate into the region, hippos revel in deepened channels, and predators, from lions to leopards, follow prey concentrated along the shrinking islands. Birds, too, flourish in astonishing numbers, from fishing herons to dazzling kingfishers.

For visitors, this means two things: boat-based exploration and breathtaking scenery. Mokoro (dugout canoe) safaris become the most intimate way to navigate the Delta, gliding past water lilies and watching the wilderness unfold in silence. Lodges that were once accessible by vehicle must now be reached by boat or light aircraft, heightening the sense of adventure.

Chobe River's Seasonal Pulse

In the far north, the Chobe River tells a different story. Here, floods arrive as the dry season tightens its grip on the interior. By June, the river swells, attracting tens of thousands of elephants—the largest concentration of these animals anywhere in Africa. Buffalo herds, antelope, and predators follow, creating one of the most spectacular wildlife gatherings on the continent.

Boat safaris along the Chobe are unmatched during this time. With animals crowding the banks, you'll see elephants wading in deep water, crocodiles basking in the sun, and hippos asserting their dominance.

Unlike the Okavango, where navigation is limited to narrow channels, the Chobe River offers wider expanses, allowing for more dramatic game viewing from the water.

The Salt Pans: From Parched Plains to Secret Lagoons

Botswana's Makgadikgadi Pans and Nxai Pan, some of the largest salt flats in the world, seem like lifeless deserts for much of the year. But when the rains arrive, these barren landscapes undergo an astonishing transformation. Shallow lakes appear where there was only dust, drawing thousands of migratory birds, including flamingos in breathtaking numbers.

The flooding also sparks the movement of zebra herds, creating one of Africa's lesser-known but equally impressive migrations. Predators, particularly lions and cheetahs, follow, making the green season an exciting time to visit these usually dry landscapes.

When to Go: Timing the Floods to Your Advantage

Your experience in Botswana will vary dramatically depending on when you visit.

- **May to October (Peak Flood in the Okavango & Chobe)**: Water levels are at their highest, making this the prime time for mokoro safaris and boat-based wildlife viewing. Large herds gather at permanent water sources, offering remarkable game-watching opportunities. This is also the driest time inland, making it the best window for traditional game drives.

- **November to April (Green Season & Rainfall Period)**: Rainfall replenishes the land, transforming dry areas into lush plains. The Okavango's water levels drop slightly, but the landscape bursts with newborn animals, birdlife, and dramatic skies. The Makgadikgadi Pans come alive, attracting flamingos and zebra migrations.

For those drawn to the rhythm of nature, the floods of Botswana offer more than just changing scenery—they dictate movement, survival, and some of the most extraordinary wildlife spectacles on Earth.

Chapter 6: The Kalahari & Beyond: Desert Adventures & Hidden Gems

Explore Botswana's mysterious sands where the San people's heritage thrives amid intimate wildlife encounters. Experience nights under countless stars and venture off familiar tracks. The Kalahari reveals quiet secrets and hidden gems, inviting you to connect with nature, savor local culture, and appreciate ancient lore in a spirited desert retreat.

The San People & Their Ancient Culture

A Legacy Etched in Time

Long before modern borders were drawn, the San people lived across the vast, sunbaked landscapes of Botswana. Their history stretches back tens of thousands of years, making them one of the oldest continuous cultures on Earth. These expert survivalists have adapted to the harsh conditions of the Kalahari, relying on their deep understanding of the land, water sources, and wildlife to thrive where few others can.

The Language of Clicks

One of the most fascinating aspects of San culture is their language, characterized by intricate click sounds. These distinct clicks, produced by the tongue and palate, set their speech apart and carry meanings that only trained ears can grasp. The most commonly spoken San languages in Botswana include Naro, !Kung, and G|ui, each rich with stories passed down through generations.

The Art of Survival in the Kalahari

San life revolves around an intimate relationship with nature. Their knowledge of plants and animals is unmatched, with each species holding medicinal, spiritual, or sustenance value. For centuries, they have relied on tracking skills so precise that they can identify an animal's age, health, and direction simply by studying footprints in the sand. Their hunting techniques involve traditional bows, poison-tipped arrows, and cooperative strategies honed over generations.

Water, a scarce resource in the Kalahari, is stored in hollowed-out ostrich eggs buried underground. These clever techniques ensure survival even in the driest months. For visitors, walking alongside a San guide provides an eye-opening experience—watching them locate hidden water, identify edible roots, and mimic bird calls with remarkable precision.

Rock Art and Storytelling

San rock paintings, found in caves and on boulders across Botswana, offer glimpses into their spiritual world. Some date back thousands of years and depict animals, hunting scenes, and trance-like ceremonies. These paintings are more than just art; they are a window into the San's connection with the spiritual realm. Many of their rituals involve dance, drumming, and chanting, often performed to heal the sick or communicate with ancestors.

Experiencing San Culture Firsthand

Several community-led cultural experiences across Botswana allow travelers to engage with the San way of life. The villages of D'Kar and Xai-Xai, as well as the Tsodilo Hills region, provide opportunities to meet San families, hear their stories, and take part in traditional activities. Visitors can learn fire-making techniques, witness trance dances, and try their hand at archery under the guidance of skilled hunters.

It's important to approach these experiences with respect. The San have faced significant challenges, including displacement from ancestral lands and loss of traditional livelihoods. Supporting ethical tourism initiatives ensures that your visit directly benefits the community while preserving their culture for future generations.

Respecting the San Way of Life

When visiting a San community, a few simple gestures go a long way in showing respect:

- **Ask before taking photos.** Many elders prefer to be asked first, as images hold deep spiritual significance in their beliefs.
- **Listen and learn.** San storytelling is an art. Sitting quietly as an elder shares wisdom is a meaningful way to connect.
- **Support local crafts.** Intricately beaded jewelry, handcrafted bows, and woven items are not just souvenirs but pieces of heritage crafted with skill and patience.

A Culture That Endures

Despite modernization, the San people continue to hold onto their traditions, adapting while maintaining their deep-rooted knowledge of the natural world. Their resilience is a testament to the strength of their identity. A visit to their communities offers more than just a glimpse into the past—it provides an opportunity to witness a way of life that has stood the test of time and still thrives in the heart of the Kalahari.

Wildlife Encounters in the Kalahari Desert

The Call of the Kalahari: An Untamed Wilderness

Vast, raw, and teeming with life, the Kalahari Desert stretches across Botswana, offering travelers a chance to experience the wild in its purest form. This semi-arid expanse is home to a remarkable array of wildlife, each species adapted to survive in its harsh but rewarding landscape. From the elusive black-maned lions to the spirited meerkats, the Kalahari's inhabitants make every visit a memorable journey into nature's resilience.

The Wildlife of the Kalahari

Black-Maned Lions

The Kalahari is famous for its powerful black-maned lions, often spotted in the Central Kalahari Game Reserve. These apex predators have adapted to the desert's dry conditions, traveling long distances in search of prey. Observing a pride in the early morning, silhouetted against the golden sands, is an unforgettable experience.

Meerkats: The Desert's Watchful Residents

Always on alert, meerkats stand like sentinels against the sunlit backdrop of the desert. These small, social creatures can often be seen scanning the horizon for predators while others dig for insects and roots. Some habituated groups allow for close viewing, making them a favorite among wildlife enthusiasts.

Brown Hyenas: The Ghosts of the Dunes

Solitary and secretive, brown hyenas roam the Kalahari under the cover of darkness. Unlike their more aggressive spotted relatives, these scavengers are shy and rarely seen. Lucky travelers who spot one near the salt pans or along the desert's edges can appreciate their role in keeping the ecosystem balanced.

Oryx and Springbok: Masters of Survival

The oryx, with its long, striking horns, embodies endurance in this extreme environment. These antelopes can go for days without drinking, extracting moisture from the plants they eat. Alongside them, springbok move gracefully in large herds, occasionally leaping into the air in a display known as pronking—possibly a way to communicate strength to predators.

Bat-Eared Foxes and Aardwolves: Nocturnal Foragers

As the sun sets, the desert awakens with lesser-known but equally fascinating creatures. Bat-eared foxes, with their oversized ears, listen keenly for termites beneath the ground, while aardwolves, distant relatives of hyenas, emerge to feast on insects, playing an essential role in pest control.

Where to See Wildlife in the Kalahari

Central Kalahari Game Reserve (CKGR)

The largest and most remote reserve in Botswana, CKGR provides a true sense of isolation. Wildlife sightings here require patience, but the rewards are immense—lions on the prowl, cheetahs scanning the horizon, and elephants appearing like mirages in the distance.

Kgalagadi Transfrontier Park

Straddling Botswana and South Africa, this protected area is known for its dramatic red dunes and remarkable predator sightings. Leopards, cheetahs, and raptors dominate the food chain here, making it a must-visit for those hoping to observe nature's raw intensity.

Deception Valley

One of the more famous areas within CKGR, Deception Valley offers seasonal transformations that attract large herds of herbivores—and, inevitably, their predators. The contrast of dry riverbeds and sparse woodlands makes this an excellent place for spotting wildlife year-round.

Best Times for Wildlife Viewing

The dry season (May to October) provides the best wildlife sightings, as animals congregate around the few remaining water sources. The cooler months (June to August) offer comfortable conditions for game drives, while the green season (November to April) brings newborn animals and vibrant birdlife.

Essential Tips for a Safe and Rewarding Experience

- **Travel with an experienced guide:** The vastness of the Kalahari makes it easy to get lost. A knowledgeable guide ensures both safety and better wildlife encounters.

- **Stay hydrated and protect yourself from the sun:** The desert climate can be unforgiving, so pack plenty of water, sunblock, and protective clothing.

- **Respect wildlife and maintain a safe distance:** While some animals may appear accustomed to human presence, they remain wild. Observing from a safe distance minimizes stress on the animals and ensures a more natural experience.

- **Bring binoculars and a camera with a zoom lens:** Many animals are best observed from afar, and the right equipment will enhance the experience without disturbing them.

Camping Under the Stars: Unforgettable Desert Nights

Few experiences compare to spending a night beneath a desert sky, where the air is crisp, the silence is deep, and the heavens stretch endlessly above. Botswana's vast landscapes, from the Makgadikgadi Pans to the Central Kalahari, offer some of the most breathtaking camping spots for those looking to sleep under the cosmos. Whether you prefer an isolated spot in the wilderness or a well-equipped site with comforts, the experience promises serenity, adventure, and a true connection with nature.

Why Camp in Botswana's Desert?

Camping in Botswana's deserts is about stepping into a world where time slows down. The landscape changes hues as the sun dips below the horizon, and when darkness falls, the stars seem close enough to touch. The Kalahari Desert and Makgadikgadi Pans provide an ideal setting for stargazing, with some of the clearest night skies in the world. Wildlife encounters are part of the magic, with nocturnal creatures emerging under the moonlight, and the distant call of a lion reminding you that this is true wilderness.

Where to Camp

Makgadikgadi Pans National Park

A seemingly endless expanse of salt flats, the Makgadikgadi Pans offer a surreal camping experience. The isolation is profound, and the starlit sky is unpolluted by artificial light. During the dry season, the land is an arid, cracked expanse, perfect for 360-degree views of the heavens. In the wet season, it transforms into a haven for wildlife, attracting flamingos, zebras, and wildebeest.

- **Camping Options:** Wild camping is allowed in designated areas, but fully serviced campsites such as Jack's Camp provide luxury under the stars.
- **Activities:** Quad biking on the pans, walking with San trackers, and spotting meerkats at sunrise.

Central Kalahari Game Reserve

One of Africa's largest protected areas, the Central Kalahari is remote and raw. Nights here bring a stillness that few places on earth can offer, with a sky so vast it feels overwhelming.

- **Camping Options:** Campsites like Piper Pan and Deception Valley cater to self-sufficient campers, while more comfortable lodges are available nearby.
- **Activities:** Night game drives to spot brown hyenas and aardwolves, as well as guided bush walks with local trackers.

Nxai Pan National Park

For those who want a mix of desert solitude and incredible wildlife, Nxai Pan delivers. The famous Baines' Baobabs stand as sentinels over this ancient land, and the open plains allow for excellent star viewing.

- **Camping Options:** Basic campsites available within the park, requiring travelers to bring their own supplies.
- **Activities:** Birdwatching, exploring ancient baobabs, and experiencing seasonal zebra migrations.

What to Pack

Camping in Botswana's deserts requires preparation. Nights can be surprisingly cold, so warm layers are essential. A good quality tent, a sleeping bag suited for desert temperatures, and a reliable headlamp are must-haves. Bring enough water, as sources are scarce, and food supplies, since many sites are far from towns. A telescope or binoculars enhances the stargazing experience, and a camera with a long exposure setting allows for capturing the brilliance of the Milky Way.

The Magic of a Desert Night

As the campfire crackles and the last embers glow, the vast silence of the desert surrounds you. The sky becomes a storybook of constellations, and the occasional rustle in the bush reminds you that life thrives even in the harshest landscapes. The experience is humbling, a rare chance to step away from modern distractions and reconnect with something ancient and enduring.

Essential Tips for a Safe and Enjoyable Experience

- **Permits & Permissions:** Many national parks require advance booking for campsites. Check regulations before heading out.

- **Wildlife Awareness:** Keep a respectful distance from animals, and never leave food exposed at night.

- **Leave No Trace:** Botswana's deserts are fragile environments. Carry out everything you bring in, and avoid disturbing the land.

- **Local Guidance:** Hiring a local guide enhances the experience, offering knowledge about the stars, the land, and the creatures that call it home.

Off-the-Beaten-Path Adventures in Botswana

For those who crave solitude, raw landscapes, and a deeper look at Botswana's wild beauty, the lesser-known corners of the country offer an experience like no other. Away from the well-trodden safari circuits, these hidden treasures reveal the untamed side of Botswana, where wildlife roams freely, traditions thrive, and nature feels untouched. If you're looking to step beyond the usual game drives and lodges, here are some extraordinary places and experiences worth seeking out.

Tsodilo Hills: The Mountain of the Gods

Why Visit?

Tsodilo Hills rises dramatically from the Kalahari sands, holding centuries of stories within its ancient rock faces. This UNESCO-listed site is home to more than 4,500 rock paintings, some dating back over 20,000 years. Revered by the San people as sacred, these hills hold spiritual significance and are often referred to as the "Louvre of the Desert."

What to See and Do

- Hike through the hills with a knowledgeable San guide who shares the legends and meanings behind the rock art.
- Watch the sunrise or sunset over the rugged terrain, where colors shift from golden hues to deep purples.
- Visit the small but insightful Tsodilo Hills Museum to learn more about the region's archaeological significance.

Getting There

The hills are located in northwestern Botswana, approximately 40 km west of Shakawe. A 4x4 vehicle is necessary to navigate the sandy tracks leading to the site.

Kubu Island: A Surreal Landscape in the Makgadikgadi

Why Visit?

Kubu Island, a granite outcrop in the heart of the Makgadikgadi Pans, is unlike any place you've seen. Surrounded by a vast salt expanse, the island is dotted with ancient baobabs, their gnarled trunks standing as silent witnesses to the passage of time. Visiting during the dry season feels like stepping onto another planet, while in the wet season, the pans transform into a shallow lake, attracting thousands of flamingos.

What to See and Do

- Walk around the island at dusk when the light casts dramatic shadows over the landscape.

- Camp under the vast sky, where the Milky Way stretches endlessly.
- Learn about the site's historical and spiritual importance to local communities.

Getting There

Kubu Island is accessible only by 4x4. The drive from Gweta or Nata takes several hours through remote terrain, so carrying extra fuel and supplies is essential.

The Okavango Delta's Remote Channels

Why Visit?

While most visitors explore the Okavango Delta by staying in luxury lodges, the more isolated channels offer an experience that feels deeply personal. Poling through narrow waterways by mokoro (traditional dugout canoe) brings you face to face with nature in its purest form. Here, the silence is broken only by the call of fish eagles and the splash of a startled hippo.

What to See and Do

- Take a guided mokoro trip through hidden lagoons and papyrus-lined channels.
- Camp on secluded islands where elephants and leopards wander by at night.
- Learn about the ecosystem from local guides whose families have lived in the delta for generations.

Getting There

Accessing the remote parts of the delta often requires a combination of light aircraft flights and boat transfers from Maun or Kasane.

Tuli Block: A Secret Safari Haven

Why Visit?

Tucked away in Botswana's eastern corner, the Tuli Block is a land of dramatic landscapes, rocky outcrops, and an abundance of wildlife. Often overlooked in favor of the Okavango and Chobe, this private reserve offers an intimate safari experience with fewer crowds.

What to See and Do

- Track elephants, lions, and cheetahs on guided bush walks or horseback safaris.
- Explore the eerie ruins of Solomon's Wall, an ancient basalt formation towering above the Motloutse River.
- Enjoy night drives where you may spot elusive nocturnal creatures like aardvarks and caracals.

Getting There

The Tuli Block is accessible via road from Gaborone (about 6 hours) or via charter flights to Limpopo Valley Airfield.

The Central Kalahari: A Desert Wilderness

Why Visit?

For those drawn to true wilderness, the Central Kalahari Game Reserve is a place of immense solitude and stark beauty. This vast reserve is home to black-maned lions, cheetahs, and the resilient San communities who have thrived in the harsh desert for thousands of years.

What to See and Do

- Take a self-drive safari through Deception Valley, where seasonal rains bring a burst of life to the desert.
- Meet San trackers who demonstrate ancient survival techniques.

- Camp beneath skies so clear you'll feel as if you can touch the stars.

Getting There

Reaching the Central Kalahari requires a sturdy 4x4, extra fuel, and careful planning. The nearest gateway is Rakops, but most visitors depart from Maun.

Practical Tips for the Adventurous Traveler

- **Pack Smart:** Many of these destinations require full self-sufficiency. Bring enough water, food, and fuel.

- **Respect Local Traditions:** Some areas are sacred to local communities—always seek permission before exploring.

- **Travel with a Guide:** Some places, like the Okavango or Tsodilo Hills, are best experienced with a knowledgeable guide.

- **Season Matters:** Dry season (May–October) is ideal for most locations, but wet season (November–April) brings unique experiences like bird migrations and lush landscapes.

- **Plan Permits in Advance:** Some areas, like the Central Kalahari and Kubu Island, require permits—organize these well ahead of time.

Chapter 7: Cities & Culture: Gaborone, Maun & Francistown

Botswana's cities each bring their own rhythm to the journey. Gaborone blends modern energy with deep-rooted traditions. Maun pulses with adventure, the last stop before the Okavango's wild beauty. Francistown carries echoes of the past, shaped by trade and migration. Markets, museums, and cultural spaces bring these stories to life.

Gaborone: The Capital's Modern Meets Traditional Charm

Overview & History

Gaborone, Botswana's capital, balances progress with tradition. Once a modest administrative center, it became the capital in 1966 when Botswana gained independence. Named after Chief Gaborone of the Batlokwa people, the city grew rapidly, shaping itself into a commercial and governmental hub. Though modernity defines its skyline, deep cultural roots are ever-present, from heritage sites to bustling local markets.

Why Visit?

Gaborone offers an easy introduction to Botswana, with its mix of city comforts and traditional heritage. It's a place where you can sip coffee in an upscale café in the morning, explore a wildlife reserve by afternoon, and end the day enjoying traditional dance under the stars. Whether it's history, culture, or nature, the city is an inviting starting point for a journey through the country.

Location & Official Information

- **Address:** Gaborone, Botswana
- **Official Website:** www.gov.bw

Best Time to Visit

Gaborone welcomes visitors year-round, but May through September (the dry season) is the most pleasant. The weather is cooler, wildlife is easier to spot, and outdoor activities are more comfortable. The city's cultural events, such as the Maitisong Festival in April, also bring an added energy.

Admission & Costs

Most city attractions, including public parks and markets, are free to enter. Museums and reserves charge a modest fee, usually between 20-100 BWP ($1.50-$7.50 USD), depending on the location.

Getting There

- **By Air:** Sir Seretse Khama International Airport (GBE) is 15 km from the city center. Direct flights connect Gaborone to Johannesburg, Cape Town, Addis Ababa, and Nairobi.
- **By Road:** Gaborone is well-linked by road, with buses from Johannesburg (5-6 hours) and Harare (12-14 hours). Car rentals are available for those wanting flexibility.
- **By Rail:** Passenger trains from Francistown and Lobatse offer an alternative for domestic travel.

Hours of Opening

Business hours generally run from **8 AM – 5 PM** on weekdays, with shorter hours on Saturdays. Government offices and some attractions close on Sundays, but malls and restaurants remain open.

What to Do & See

- **Gaborone Game Reserve:** A small but rewarding park with zebra, warthogs, and over 200 bird species.
- **Three Dikgosi Monument:** Honoring Botswana's founding chiefs, this site offers insights into the country's history.
- **Botswana National Museum:** Exhibits on local art, history, and culture.
- **Kgale Hill:** A hike to the top rewards visitors with sweeping views of the city.
- **Mokolodi Nature Reserve:** Just outside town, this reserve is home to rhinos, giraffes, and cheetahs.
- **Main Mall & Central Business District:** Ideal for shopping, local crafts, and casual dining.

Nearby Restaurants & Attractions

- **Sanitas Tea Garden:** A tranquil café set within a plant nursery, known for fresh food and a relaxing setting.
- **Bulls & Broncos:** A lively steakhouse serving Botswana beef.
- **No. 1 Ladies' Detective Agency Tour:** Fans of Alexander McCall Smith's books can visit sites linked to the famous series.
- **Gaborone Dam:** Popular for picnics, birdwatching, and water activities.

Photography Tips

- Sunrise and sunset at **Kgale Hill** create dramatic lighting over the city.
- The **Three Dikgosi Monument** is best photographed in the late afternoon when shadows are softer.

- **Mokolodi's wildlife** is most active in the early morning or just before sunset.
- Cityscapes from **Gaborone Dam** capture both nature and urban life in one frame.

Laws & Rules

- **Wildlife Protection:** Do not feed or disturb animals in reserves.
- **Photography Restrictions:** Avoid taking photos of government buildings and military areas.
- **Alcohol Laws:** Sales are restricted after 7 PM on weekdays and after 2 PM on Sundays.
- **Traffic Rules:** Drive on the left side; seat belts are mandatory.

Practical Information

- **Currency:** Botswana Pula (BWP)
- **Language:** English and Setswana
- **Emergency Numbers:** Police: 999 | Ambulance: 997
- **Internet & Connectivity:** Free Wi-Fi is available in major malls and hotels.

GPS & Navigation

- **Gaborone Game Reserve:** -24.6690, 25.9351
- **Three Dikgosi Monument:** -24.6546, 25.9085
- **Kgale Hill:** -24.6920, 25.8836
- **Mokolodi Nature Reserve:** -24.7512, 25.8080

Interesting Facts

- Gaborone was a small village before being chosen as Botswana's capital.

- The city was named after Chief Gaborone, but locals often refer to it as 'Gabs.'

- Botswana's first-ever traffic lights were installed here in the 1990s.

- Parts of the TV adaptation of The No. 1 Ladies' Detective Agency were filmed on location.

Maun: The Gateway to the Delta & Adventure Hub

Overview & History

Maun, the lively entry point to Botswana's Okavango Delta, has grown from a dusty frontier town into a thriving hub for explorers and wildlife enthusiasts. Founded in 1915 as the capital of the Batawana people, it was historically a center for cattle trading. Over time, it has transformed into a base for safaris, flights over the Delta, and cultural encounters. While modern amenities have arrived, Maun retains a rugged, untamed feel, making it an exciting stop before heading into the wilderness.

Why Visit Maun?

Maun serves as the perfect balance between civilization and the raw beauty of Botswana's landscapes. It offers access to the Delta's intricate waterways, wildlife encounters, and a chance to experience local culture. Whether you're looking for a thrilling safari, a scenic flight over vast floodplains, or a relaxed evening along the Thamalakane River, Maun provides an excellent starting point.

Location & Official Information

- **Coordinates:** 19.9953° S, 23.4181° E
- **Official Website:** Botswana Tourism

Best Time to Visit

The ideal time depends on the experience you're after:

- **Dry Season (May - October):** Best for wildlife viewing as animals gather around water sources. The Okavango Delta floods during this period, creating breathtaking landscapes perfect for mokoro (canoe) trips.
- **Wet Season (November - April):** Lush scenery, birdwatching at its finest, and fewer crowds. However, some areas may be difficult to access due to heavy rains.

Admission Tickets & Entry Fees

There's no fee to enter Maun, but excursions into the Okavango Delta, Moremi Game Reserve, or private concessions require permits or guided tours. Prices vary based on activities and locations:

- **Moremi Game Reserve Entry Fee:** Approx. $10 per person
- **Mokoro Excursions:** Starting at $50 per person
- **Scenic Flights:** Around $120 per person for a 45-minute flight

Getting to Maun

- **By Air:** Maun International Airport (MUB) is the primary entry point, with flights from Gaborone, Johannesburg, and Cape Town.
- **By Road:** The A3 highway connects Maun to Nata (300 miles) and Gaborone (600 miles). Self-driving is possible but requires a 4x4 for remote areas.
- **By Bus:** Long-distance buses run between Maun and Gaborone, but journeys can take over 10 hours.

Hours of Operation

Maun operates year-round, but specific businesses, attractions, and parks have their own schedules. Most tour operators function daily, though early booking is recommended during peak season.

Closest Town

Maun itself is the nearest town, serving as the supply and logistics center for the Okavango Delta and northern Botswana.

Things to Do & See

- **Scenic Flights Over the Delta** – Witness the Okavango's vast waterways from the air.
- **Mokoro Canoe Safari** – Glide through channels in a traditional dugout canoe, guided by a local poler.
- **Moremi Game Reserve** – One of Africa's best wildlife areas, home to lions, elephants, leopards, and wild dogs.
- **Nhabe Museum** – Learn about Botswana's history, art, and indigenous cultures.
- **Thamalakane River Sunset Cruises** – A relaxing way to end the day with birdwatching and cool breezes.
- **Helicopter Rides** – Perfect for aerial photography with doors-off flights available.

Where to Eat

- **The Tshilli Farmstall** – Known for organic food, fresh juices, and a relaxed atmosphere.
- **Dusty Donkey Café** – Serves excellent coffee and homemade cakes.
- **Riverside Bistro** – Ideal for a meal with a view, featuring fresh fish and local dishes.

- **French Connection** – A mix of international and local flavors, including grilled meats and seafood.
- **The Red Monkey Lodge** – Offers great pizza and a friendly vibe.

Nearby Attractions

- **Boro Village** – Experience traditional Botswana culture and local crafts.
- **Maun Wildlife Educational Park** – A small but informative park showcasing native animals.
- **Tsodilo Hills** (4 hours away) – A UNESCO World Heritage site featuring ancient rock paintings.

Photography Tips

- **Golden Hour Magic:** Early mornings and late afternoons provide the best light for landscapes and wildlife.
- **Aerial Views:** A polarizing filter enhances contrast when capturing the Delta from above.
- **Water Reflections:** The calm channels of the Okavango create mirror-like surfaces, perfect for reflections.
- **Wildlife Patience:** Keep a zoom lens handy for capturing animals without disturbing them.

Laws & Rules to Follow

- **Respect Wildlife:** Keep a safe distance, never feed animals, and avoid loud noises.
- **No Off-Road Driving:** Straying from designated routes in protected areas can harm the environment.
- **Drone Restrictions:** A special permit is required for drone usage.

- **Cultural Sensitivity:** Ask permission before photographing locals.
- **Park Entry Permits:** Ensure you have the necessary documentation when visiting reserves.

Practical Information

- **Currency:** Botswana Pula (BWP)
- **ATMs:** Available in Maun, but cash is recommended for remote areas.
- **Language:** English is widely spoken, but Setswana is the national language.
- **Medical:** Maun has clinics, but travel insurance covering medical evacuation is recommended.
- **Electricity:** 220-240V with British-style plugs.

GPS & Navigation

- **Maun Airport:** -19.9728, 23.4293
- **Moremi Game Reserve Gate:** -19.4333, 23.5833
- **Thamalakane Riverfront:** -19.9833, 23.4167

Interesting Facts

- The Okavango Delta is one of the only inland deltas in the world, draining into the Kalahari Desert rather than the ocean.
- Maun means "the place of reeds" in the language of the BaYei people.
- The airport runway in Maun is one of the busiest in Africa due to the high volume of charter flights heading into the Delta.
- A herd of elephants once casually strolled through Maun's main road—proof that the wild is never too far away!

Francistown: A Historical and Cultural Crossroads

Overview and History

Francistown, Botswana's second-largest city, stands at the crossroads of history and modern life. This vibrant hub was once a key center during the gold rush of the late 19th century, drawing prospectors from around the world. Named after Daniel Francis, an early gold prospector, the city flourished as a commercial and cultural melting pot, shaped by its mining heritage and the trade routes that connected it to the rest of Southern Africa. Today, Francistown remains a gateway to Botswana's north, offering a glimpse into the past while embracing the present.

Why Visit Francistown?

For travelers interested in history, culture, and everyday life in Botswana, Francistown provides a fascinating experience. The city's museums, markets, and historical sites offer a window into its rich past, while its lively streets reflect the warmth of its people. Whether you're passing through on a journey to the Okavango Delta or seeking a deeper understanding of Botswana's mining heritage, Francistown is worth a stop.

Location and How to Get There

Francistown is located in eastern Botswana, near the border with Zimbabwe.

- **Address:** Central Francistown, Botswana
- **GPS Coordinates:** -21.1731, 27.5124
- **Nearest Town:** Tonota (about 35 km away)

- **Official Website:** No dedicated tourism website, but general information can be found on the Botswana Tourism Organization site.

- **How to Get There:**
    - **By Air:** Francistown International Airport (FRW) connects the city with Gaborone and other regional hubs.
    - **By Road:** The A1 highway links Francistown to Gaborone (about 435 km away) and Zimbabwe's Plumtree border post (about 90 km away).
    - **By Bus:** Regular buses run between Francistown, Gaborone, and Bulawayo, Zimbabwe.

Best Time to Visit

Francistown has a semi-arid climate, with hot summers and mild winters.

- **May to August (Cool, Dry Season):** Ideal for sightseeing, as daytime temperatures remain comfortable.
- **September to April (Hot, Rainy Season):** Warmer temperatures with occasional heavy rains, but a great time for experiencing the city's vibrant markets and local events.

Admission and Opening Hours

Most attractions in Francistown are open year-round, though hours may vary.

- **Supa Ngwao Museum:**
    - **Admission:** Free (donations encouraged)
    - **Hours:** Monday to Friday, 9 AM – 5 PM; Saturday, 9 AM – 1 PM; Closed Sundays

- **Domboshaba Ruins:**
  - **Admission:** P20 for adults, P10 for children
  - **Hours:** Open daily from sunrise to sunset

Things to Do and See

Supa Ngwao Museum

A must-visit for history enthusiasts, this museum showcases artifacts from Francistown's mining days, traditional crafts, and stories of the Kalanga people who have lived in the area for centuries.

Domboshaba Ruins

Just outside the city, these ancient stone ruins offer a glimpse into a civilization that thrived centuries ago. The remnants of a walled settlement, built by ancestors of the Kalanga people, provide insight into the region's historical significance.

Tachila Nature Reserve

Located a short drive from Francistown, this reserve offers walking trails, wildlife viewing, and peaceful landscapes, perfect for those looking to experience Botswana's natural beauty outside the city.

Nyangabgwe Hill

A great spot for panoramic views of the city, especially at sunrise or sunset. Local legends and historical accounts add depth to its significance.

Where to Eat

Francistown has a mix of local and international flavors, from casual eateries to upscale restaurants.

- **Thorn Tree Café:** A local favorite for breakfast and coffee.
- **Barbara's Bistro:** Known for its home-cooked meals and welcoming atmosphere.

- **Digger's Inn Restaurant:** Offers a blend of local and international cuisine, inspired by the city's mining history.
- **Merilicious:** Great for traditional Botswana dishes, including seswaa (shredded beef) and pap (maize porridge).

Nearby Attractions

- **Shashe Dam:** A peaceful spot for birdwatching and picnics, about 30 minutes from Francistown.
- **Sebina Hot Springs:** Located about an hour away, these natural hot springs are a relaxing getaway.
- **Matopos National Park (Zimbabwe):** Just across the border, this UNESCO-listed park is worth a visit for those heading into Zimbabwe.

Photography Tips

- **Golden Hour:** Capture the best shots of Nyangabgwe Hill and Domboshaba Ruins at sunrise or sunset.
- **Markets:** The bustling central market provides colorful backdrops of daily life.
- **Wildlife:** If visiting Tachila Nature Reserve, bring a zoom lens for animal photography.

Laws and Practical Information

- **Currency:** Botswana Pula (BWP)
- **Language:** English is widely spoken, though Setswana and Kalanga are commonly used.
- **Electricity:** 230V, Type D and M plugs (same as South Africa)
- **Driving:** Left-hand side of the road; an international driver's license is recommended.

- **Safety:** Francistown is generally safe, but as in any city, avoid walking alone at night in unfamiliar areas.
- **Health:** It is advisable to take malaria precautions, especially in the wet season.

Interesting Facts

- Francistown was Botswana's first real city, developing long before Gaborone became the capital.
- The city's gold rush history is still visible in some abandoned mines surrounding the area.
- The name "Francistown" comes from Daniel Francis, but the area has been home to the Kalanga people for centuries before European settlement.

Best Museums, Markets & Cultural Experiences

1. Botswana National Museum and Art Gallery

Located in the heart of Gaborone, the Botswana National Museum and Art Gallery serves as a cornerstone for preserving the nation's history and culture. Established in 1967, it showcases traditional crafts, artworks, and historical artifacts that narrate Botswana's story.

- **Contact Information:** Independence Avenue, Gaborone, Botswana.
- **When to Go:** Open year-round; consider visiting during weekdays to avoid crowds.
- **How to Get There:** Easily accessible by taxi or public transport within Gaborone.

- **Opening Hours:** Typically open from 8:00 AM to 4:30 PM, Monday through Friday.
- **What to Expect:** Diverse exhibits including traditional crafts, paintings, and historical artifacts.
- **What to Bring:** Camera, notepad, and a curious mind.
- **Prices:** Nominal entrance fee; approximately 10-20 BWP.
- **Tips:** Guided tours are available and enhance the experience.

2. Kuru Art Project

Nestled in the village of D'Kar, the Kuru Art Project is a community-driven initiative that highlights the artistic talents of the San people. Visitors can admire and purchase unique artworks that reflect the rich traditions and stories of the San community.

- **Contact Information:** D'Kar Village, Ghanzi District, Botswana.
- **When to Go:** Open throughout the year; visiting during local festivals offers a deeper insight.
- **How to Get There:** Accessible via road; it's advisable to hire a local guide or driver.
- **Opening Hours:** Generally open from 9:00 AM to 5:00 PM.
- **What to Expect:** Authentic San art, including paintings and crafts.
- **What to Bring:** Cash for purchases, as card facilities may be limited.
- **Prices:** Art pieces vary in price; supporting local artists directly benefits the community.
- **Tips:** Engage with the artists to learn the stories behind their creations.

3. Maun Immersive Cultural Tour

Maun, often considered the gateway to the Okavango Delta, offers immersive cultural tours that provide a window into the daily lives of local communities. These tours often include visits to traditional homes, schools, and markets.

- **Contact Information:** Various tour operators in Maun; it's best to book through reputable agencies.
- **When to Go:** Dry season (April to October) is ideal for travel.
- **How to Get There:** Maun is accessible by air and road; tours typically start from the town center.
- **Opening Hours:** Tours usually run during daylight hours; specific times depend on the operator.
- **What to Expect:** Engaging interactions with locals, traditional dance performances, and insights into daily life.
- **What to Bring:** Comfortable walking shoes, sun protection, and a respectful attitude.
- **Prices:** Tour prices vary; expect to pay around 500-800 BWP per person.
- **Tips:** Booking in advance ensures availability; consider small group tours for a more personalized experience.

4. Gaborone Craft Market

Situated in the bustling city of Gaborone, the Craft Market is a vibrant spot where artisans showcase their handmade goods, including basketry, pottery, and beadwork. It's an excellent place to find unique souvenirs and support local craftsmen.

- **Contact Information:** Main Mall, Gaborone, Botswana.
- **When to Go:** Weekends are particularly lively, with more vendors present.

- **How to Get There:** Located in the city center; easily reachable by taxi or on foot if you're nearby.
- **Opening Hours:** Typically from 8:00 AM to 5:00 PM.
- **What to Expect:** A variety of stalls selling handcrafted items.
- **What to Bring:** Cash, as not all vendors accept cards.
- **Prices:** Prices vary; haggling is common, but always fair.
- **Tips:** Engage with vendors to learn about the crafts; purchasing directly supports their livelihoods.

5. Okavango Delta Cultural Experience

Beyond its natural splendor, the Okavango Delta offers cultural experiences that allow visitors to connect with indigenous communities. Participate in traditional activities, learn about local customs, and appreciate the harmonious relationship between the people and their environment.

- **Contact Information:** Various tour operators offer cultural experiences; research and choose one that collaborates closely with local communities.
- **When to Go:** The dry season (May to October) offers easier access and comfortable weather.
- **How to Get There:** Access is typically via Maun, with tours providing transport into the delta.
- **Opening Hours:** Tours are scheduled; consult with your chosen operator.
- **What to Expect:** Canoe trips, village visits, and storytelling sessions.
- **What to Bring:** Insect repellent, comfortable clothing, and an open heart.

- **Prices:** Prices vary based on the length and inclusions of the tour; multi-day experiences may start

Chapter 8: Luxury Lodges, Eco-Stays & Budget-Friendly Accommodations

From luxury lodges overlooking the savannah to cozy guesthouses in lively villages, Botswana has stays to match every traveler's style. Whether you're seeking an elegant safari retreat, a mid-range boutique hotel, a budget-friendly campsite, or an eco-conscious escape, each option offers comfort, character, and a deeper connection to the land.

Top Luxury Safari Lodges & Resorts

Botswana is home to some of the most spectacular safari lodges in Africa, offering unmatched access to breathtaking landscapes and incredible wildlife encounters. Whether you're seeking a private retreat on the banks of the Okavango Delta or an exclusive lodge deep in the Kalahari, there are plenty of exceptional stays to choose from. Here's a detailed guide to some of the finest luxury safari lodges and resorts in Botswana.

1. Mombo Camp

Description:

Mombo Camp sits in the heart of the Okavango Delta, an area famous for its high concentration of wildlife. This ultra-luxurious camp offers elevated tents with sweeping views of floodplains teeming with game. The camp operates with a strong commitment to conservation, ensuring an authentic and responsible safari experience.

Official Website:

https://www.wildernessdestinations.com

Property Amenities:
- Private plunge pools
- Spa and wellness treatments
- Fine dining with locally sourced ingredients
- Expert-guided game drives and walking safaris
- Photography hides

Room Features:
- Spacious en-suite tents with open-air showers
- Expansive decks with daybeds
- Indoor and outdoor lounging areas
- Solar-powered air conditioning
- Complimentary minibar

Room Types:
- Luxury Tented Suites
- Private Villa (available on request)

Pros & Cons:

Pros:
- Unparalleled wildlife viewing
- Exclusive, intimate experience with limited guests
- Exceptional hospitality and gourmet dining

Cons:
- Expensive, catering to high-end travelers
- Limited availability due to demand

Location:

Situated in Moremi Game Reserve, within the Okavango Delta.

How to Get There:

- Fly into Maun International Airport (MUB)
- Take a charter flight to Mombo Airstrip, followed by a short drive to camp

Check-In & Check-Out:

- Check-in: 2:00 PM
- Check-out: 10:00 AM

Nearby Attractions:

- Chief's Island
- Moremi Game Reserve
- Birdwatching along the delta

Price Range:

Starting from $2,500 per person per night (all-inclusive)

Contact Information:

- Phone: +27 11 807 1800
- Email: reservations@wildernessdestinations.com

2. Zarafa Camp

Description:

Located in the private Selinda Reserve, Zarafa Camp is an exclusive eco-friendly lodge known for its incredible big-game sightings and ultra-personalized service. With only a few luxury tents, the camp ensures privacy and tranquility.

Official Website:

https://greatplainsconservation.com

Property Amenities:

- Private plunge pools with views of the lagoon
- Gourmet dining under the stars
- Outdoor gym and yoga deck
- Exclusive use of Swarovski binoculars and professional cameras

Room Features:

- Oversized copper bathtubs
- Expansive wooden decks
- Wood-burning stoves for chilly nights
- Private dining areas

Room Types:

- Luxury Tented Suites
- Private 2-Bedroom Suite

Pros & Cons:

Pros:

- Small and intimate setting
- Excellent game viewing, including lions and elephants
- Exceptional, personalized service

Cons:

- Remote location requires multiple flights
- Premium pricing

Location:

Situated in Selinda Reserve, Northern Botswana.

How to Get There:

- Fly into Maun International Airport (MUB)
- Take a charter flight to Selinda Airstrip, followed by a short drive to camp

Check-In & Check-Out:

- Check-in: 2:00 PM
- Check-out: 10:00 AM

Nearby Attractions:

- Selinda Spillway
- Boating safaris on the Linyanti River

Price Range:

Starting from $2,300 per person per night (all-inclusive)

Contact Information:

- Phone: +27 87 354 6591
- Email: reservations@greatplainsconservation.com

3. Sandibe Okavango Safari Lodge

Description:

Nestled in the Okavango Delta, Sandibe Okavango Safari Lodge combines luxury with a deep connection to nature. The lodge's organic design blends seamlessly into its surroundings, offering a tranquil retreat amid lush wilderness.

Official Website:

https://www.andbeyond.com

Property Amenities:

- Infinity pool overlooking the delta
- Open-air boma dining
- Private butler service
- Daily guided safaris and mokoro (canoe) rides

Room Features:

- Handcrafted interiors inspired by the Delta's ecosystem
- Outdoor showers
- Floor-to-ceiling glass walls
- Private decks with plunge pools

Room Types:

- Luxury Suites
- Family Suites

Pros & Cons:

Pros:

- Unique, eco-conscious design

- Outstanding service and guiding
- Excellent location for year-round game viewing

Cons:
- Can be difficult to book due to high demand
- Pricing is on the higher end

Location:

Located in a private concession in the Okavango Delta.

How to Get There:
- Fly into Maun International Airport (MUB)
- Take a short charter flight to Chitabe Airstrip, followed by a 45-minute drive to the lodge

Check-In & Check-Out:
- Check-in: 2:00 PM
- Check-out: 11:00 AM

Nearby Attractions:
- Okavango Delta waterways
- Birdwatching safaris
- Seasonal fishing excursions

Price Range:

Starting from $1,900 per person per night (all-inclusive)

Contact Information:
- Phone: +27 11 809 4300
- Email: safaris@andbeyond.com

Mid-Range & Boutique Hotels for a Comfortable Stay

Cresta Maun Hotel

Description: Nestled on the banks of the Thamalakane River, Cresta Maun Hotel offers a relaxed stay with easy access to the Okavango Delta. The property blends contemporary African design with warm hospitality, making it an excellent stop for travelers heading into the wilderness or those just looking to unwind.

Official Website: https://www.crestahotels.com

Property Amenities:

- Outdoor swimming pool
- Restaurant and bar with river views
- Fitness center
- Free Wi-Fi
- Conference facilities
- Airport shuttle (additional charge)

Room Features:

- Air conditioning
- Private balconies (in select rooms)
- Satellite TV
- Work desk and seating area
- Tea and coffee facilities

Room Types:

- Standard Double Room
- Deluxe River View Room
- Executive Suite

Pros:
✓ Convenient location for accessing Moremi Game Reserve
✓ Clean, well-maintained rooms
✓ Friendly and accommodating staff

Cons:
✗ Can be busy during peak season
✗ Some rooms may experience noise from the nearby road

Location: Maun, Botswana
How to Get There: A 15-minute drive from Maun International Airport. Taxis and car rentals are readily available.
Check-in/Check-out: 2:00 PM / 11:00 AM
Nearby Attractions: Okavango Delta, Nhabe Museum, Maun Game Reserve
Price Range: $100 – $180 per night
Contact: +267 686 3128

Gweta Lodge

Description: Situated near the Makgadikgadi Pans, Gweta Lodge provides a cozy, relaxed atmosphere with traditional African décor and a welcoming feel. It's ideal for travelers looking to explore the vast salt pans and experience the natural beauty of Botswana.

Official Website: https://www.gwetalodge.com

Property Amenities:

- Swimming pool
- Restaurant and bar
- Guided safari tours
- Free parking
- Lounge area

Room Features:

- Mosquito nets
- En-suite bathrooms
- Ceiling fans
- Rustic African-inspired furnishings

Room Types:

- Standard Chalet
- Family Chalet
- Safari Tents

Pros:

✓ Unique, immersive setting near the salt pans
✓ Excellent on-site guides for safari excursions
✓ Friendly, laid-back atmosphere

Cons:

✗ Limited Wi-Fi connectivity
✗ Remote location—requires planning for transport

Location: Gweta, Botswana
How to Get There: Located about 2 hours from Maun by road. The lodge can arrange transport.

Check-in/Check-out: 2:00 PM / 10:00 AM
Nearby Attractions: Makgadikgadi Pans, Ntwetwe Pan, Baines' Baobabs
Price Range: $80 – $160 per night
Contact: +267 7232 8227

Indaba Lodge Gaborone

Description: A modern, well-equipped lodge located in Botswana's capital city, Indaba Lodge Gaborone offers comfort with a stylish touch. It caters to both business and leisure travelers, providing convenience and thoughtful service.

Official Website: https://www.indabalodge.com

Property Amenities:

- Outdoor swimming pool
- Fitness center
- Restaurant and coffee shop
- Conference and business facilities
- 24-hour front desk

Room Features:

- Air-conditioned rooms
- Flat-screen TV with satellite channels
- Mini-fridge
- Safe deposit box
- Desk and ergonomic chair

Room Types:

- Standard Room
- Deluxe King Room
- Executive Suite

Pros:
✓ Central location with easy access to shopping and dining
✓ Reliable Wi-Fi
✓ Professional and courteous staff

Cons:
✗ Some rooms can be small
✗ Noise from surrounding city streets

Location: Gaborone, Botswana
How to Get There: About 15 minutes from Sir Seretse Khama International Airport. Taxis and ride services are available.
Check-in/Check-out: 2:00 PM / 11:00 AM
Nearby Attractions: National Museum and Art Gallery, Mokolodi Nature Reserve, Three Dikgosi Monument
Price Range: $90 – $200 per night
Contact: +267 391 5800

Budget Hostels, Campsites & Guesthouses

Traveling through Botswana doesn't have to drain your wallet. Whether you're a backpacker, an adventure-seeker, or simply looking for an affordable stay, the country has plenty of options. From cozy guesthouses to campsites with breathtaking views, you can enjoy comfort and convenience without spending too much. Here's a rundown of budget-friendly accommodations, including key details to help you plan your trip.

The Elephant Trail Hostel & Campsite

Location: Maun, Botswana

Website: www.elephanttrail.com

Contact: +267 68 65 432 | info@elephanttrail.com

Price Range: $15–$50 per night

Property Amenities:

- Free Wi-Fi in common areas
- Shared kitchen and BBQ facilities
- Outdoor seating and campfire area
- Laundry service (additional cost)
- Secure parking

Room Features:

- Dormitory beds with personal lockers
- Private safari tents with basic furniture
- Thatched-roof bungalows with en-suite bathrooms

Room Types:

- Mixed and female-only dormitories
- Private double and twin rooms
- Camping sites with access to shared facilities

Pros:

✓ Great social atmosphere for travelers
✓ Close to Moremi Game Reserve
✓ Budget-friendly meal options
✓ Helpful staff for booking safaris and activities

Cons:

✗ Can get noisy due to communal areas
✗ Limited availability during peak season

How to Get There:

From Maun Airport, take a taxi (around 10 minutes). Shared shuttle services are also available.

Nearby Attractions:

- Moremi Game Reserve (1-hour drive)
- Okavango Delta boat tours (organizable from hostel)
- Nhabe Museum (15-minute walk)

Check-In & Check-Out:

- Check-in: 2:00 PM
- Check-out: 11:00 AM

The Old House Guesthouse

Location: Kasane, Botswana

Website: www.oldhousebotswana.com

Contact: +267 71 23 4567 | bookings@oldhousebotswana.com

Price Range: $40–$80 per night

Property Amenities:

- On-site restaurant & bar
- Small swimming pool
- Complimentary breakfast
- Free bicycle rentals
- Wi-Fi in rooms and common areas

Room Features:

- Air-conditioned rooms
- Mosquito nets & ceiling fans
- En-suite bathrooms
- Mini-fridge & tea-making facilities

Room Types:

- Standard twin and double rooms
- Family rooms with extra bedding

Pros:

✓ Great location near Chobe National Park
✓ Friendly and knowledgeable staff
✓ Cozy and relaxing environment
✓ Convenient for booking boat safaris and game drives

Cons:

✗ Limited budget options for food
✗ Small rooms compared to larger hotels

How to Get There:

From Kasane Airport, it's a 5-minute taxi ride. The guesthouse can arrange pickups upon request.

Nearby Attractions:

- Chobe National Park (5-minute drive)
- Chobe River boat cruises (organized on-site)
- Local craft market (10-minute walk)

Check-In & Check-Out:

- Check-in: 1:00 PM
- Check-out: 10:00 AM

Kalahari Sands Backpackers

Location: Ghanzi, Botswana

Website: www.kalaharisands.com

Contact: +267 77 45 3210 | reservations@kalaharisands.com

Price Range: $12–$45 per night

Property Amenities:

- Communal lounge & outdoor firepit
- Self-catering kitchen
- Guided Bushmen cultural walks (extra charge)
- Wi-Fi in main areas
- Free coffee & tea station

Room Features:

- Simple but clean dorms & private rooms
- Shared bathrooms with hot showers
- Mosquito netting provided
- Camping spaces available

Room Types:

- 6-bed dormitories
- Private twin & double rooms
- Camping plots with access to common facilities

Pros:

✓ Affordable rates
✓ Cultural tours available
✓ Relaxed and laid-back atmosphere
✓ Located along the route to the Central Kalahari

Cons:

✗ Basic facilities—no luxury options
✗ Can get dusty due to desert surroundings

How to Get There:

From Ghanzi Airport, take a taxi (about 10 minutes). Public buses from Maun or Windhoek also stop nearby.

Nearby Attractions:

- Bushmen cultural villages (organized from the hostel)
- Ghanzi Craft Market (10-minute drive)
- Central Kalahari Game Reserve (3-hour drive)

Check-In & Check-Out:
- Check-in: 3:00 PM
- Check-out: 10:30 AM

Botswana's budget-friendly accommodations make it easy to explore the country without breaking the bank. Whether you're soaking in the culture, heading out for a safari, or just looking for a quiet place to rest, these hostels, campsites, and guesthouses have you covered.

Unique Eco-Friendly & Sustainable Stays

Botswana is known for its vast landscapes, abundant wildlife, and deep-rooted conservation efforts. Staying in accommodations that align with the country's commitment to sustainability allows travelers to experience nature without leaving a heavy footprint. From solar-powered safari lodges to community-run eco-camps, these stays blend comfort with responsible tourism, ensuring that each visit contributes positively to the land and the people who call it home.

Solar-Powered Safari Lodges

Many lodges across Botswana have adopted solar energy, reducing reliance on diesel generators and minimizing environmental impact. These accommodations are designed to merge with the surroundings, offering breathtaking views without disrupting the natural ecosystem.

- **Camp Kalahari** (Makgadikgadi Pans): Nestled among palm trees, this camp runs on solar power and uses natural ventilation to keep rooms cool. The tents are built on raised platforms, reducing their impact on the fragile salt pans. Activities include walking with the Zu/'hoasi Bushmen and watching the annual zebra migration.

- **Duba Plains Camp** (Okavango Delta): A leader in sustainable luxury, this camp operates on 100% solar energy and supports conservation projects focused on lions and elephants. Elevated wooden walkways reduce land disturbance, while locally sourced materials give the structures an authentic touch.
- **Chobe Game Lodge** (Chobe National Park): The only permanent lodge inside Chobe National Park, this stay is fully eco-certified. Electric safari vehicles and solar-powered boats offer a quieter, more immersive experience, allowing guests to observe wildlife without the hum of diesel engines.

Community-Run Eco-Camps

Staying at a community-owned lodge directly supports local people, ensuring that tourism benefits those who have safeguarded these lands for generations. These camps focus on cultural exchange, sustainability, and conservation.

- **Ghoha Hills Savuti Lodge** (Savuti, Chobe National Park): Owned and operated by the local community, this lodge provides employment and training for nearby villages. Solar panels supply energy, and water is sourced responsibly to avoid depleting local reserves.
- **Gomoti Plains Camp** (Okavango Delta): This low-impact camp blends traditional craftsmanship with modern eco-design. Materials are locally sourced, and wastewater is treated and repurposed. Guests can enjoy guided walks led by community members who share knowledge passed down through generations.
- **Moremi Crossing** (Moremi Game Reserve): Built with biodegradable materials and powered by solar, this camp minimizes its effect on the environment. Locally produced furniture and decor celebrate the region's culture while ensuring a minimal carbon footprint.

Low-Impact Mobile Camps

For those seeking adventure without permanent structures, mobile camps provide a way to experience Botswana's wilderness without leaving lasting traces.

- **Letaka Safaris**: This mobile safari operator specializes in lightweight, eco-conscious camps that move across the Delta and Central Kalahari. Tents are pitched only for short stays, and waste is carried out, leaving nature undisturbed.
- **Okavango Horse Safaris**: Combining horseback riding with mobile camping, this operation moves through pristine areas where vehicles cannot reach. Portable solar showers and compostable toilets ensure comfort without harming the environment.
- **Bush Ways Mobile Safaris**: Offering guided safaris with small ecological footprints, this mobile camp provides bucket showers, solar lighting, and biodegradable products, ensuring the wilderness remains unspoiled.

Lodges with Innovative Water Conservation

Water is a precious resource in Botswana, especially in arid regions. Some lodges have developed innovative ways to conserve water while maintaining comfort for guests.

- **Kwetsani Camp** (Okavango Delta): Rainwater collection systems and greywater recycling reduce water waste. Raised decks and wooden pathways prevent disruption to wetlands, allowing wildlife to move freely beneath.
- **Jack's Camp** (Makgadikgadi Pans): Uses deep borehole water rather than drawing from nearby rivers, ensuring natural water sources remain untouched. Guest showers use a unique low-flow system that reduces water usage without sacrificing comfort.

- **Zarafa Camp** (Selinda Reserve): The first camp in Botswana to use a completely closed water recycling system. Every drop is filtered and reused where possible, and energy-efficient cooling methods help reduce water consumption.

Eco-Luxury: Sustainability Meets Comfort

For travelers who want a high-end experience while maintaining environmental responsibility, these lodges blend luxury with conservation.

- **Sandibe Okavango Safari Lodge** (Okavango Delta): This lodge is built from sustainable timber and inspired by pangolin scales, seamlessly integrating into its surroundings. Private plunge pools use filtered water, and the entire lodge is run on solar power.

- **Selinda Camp** (Selinda Reserve): A small, exclusive camp that runs on solar energy and sources food from local farmers. The lodge funds anti-poaching efforts and offers conservation-focused experiences.

- **Vumbura Plains** (Okavango Delta): Combining local craftsmanship with modern sustainability, this lodge features furniture made from reclaimed wood and a no-single-use-plastics policy. The camp supports local communities through education and conservation programs.

How to Choose the Right Stay

Selecting an eco-friendly stay in Botswana depends on personal travel preferences, whether it's a solar-powered lodge, a community-run camp, or a mobile safari. Consider:

- **Impact on Local Communities**: Opt for stays that employ and support local people.

- **Energy and Water Use**: Look for solar power, rainwater collection, and water conservation measures.

- **Wildlife Protection**: Choose lodges that actively participate in conservation efforts.
- **Waste Management**: Seek accommodations that minimize waste, eliminate plastic, and use biodegradable products.

Chapter 9: Food & Dining: A Taste of Botswana's Culinary Delights

Botswana's flavors tell a story of tradition, community, and the land itself. From slow-cooked seswaa to spicy mopane worms, each bite carries a sense of place. Savor meals in local eateries, under a starlit sky, or at bustling markets. Here's where to find the best meals and unforgettable dining experiences.

Traditional Dishes You Must Try

Botswana's food is a reflection of its landscapes, traditions, and the warmth of its people. Meals are prepared with care, using time-honored techniques that bring out deep, satisfying flavors. Whether enjoyed in a family home, at a roadside stall, or in a lively market, these dishes offer a taste of everyday life.

Seswaa – The Soul of Botswana's Cuisine

Main Ingredients & Flavors: Beef (or goat), salt, water. Cooked slowly until tender, then shredded into flavorful, juicy strands. Traditionally served with **bogobe** (sorghum porridge) or **phaleche** (maize porridge).

Estimated Budget: 50–120 BWP ($4–$9) per serving.

Where to Find It (GPS Locations):

- **Bull & Bush, Gaborone** (GPS: -24.6577, 25.9081)
- **Motsana Arts Café, Maun** (GPS: -19.9834, 23.4181)
- **Mokoro Lodge, Maun** (GPS: -19.9949, 23.4187)

Preparation: Large cuts of meat are simmered for hours over low heat, using only salt for seasoning. Once tender, it's pounded into fine shreds using wooden paddles.

Taste Profile: Rich, meaty, and deeply savory. The slow cooking process concentrates the flavors, creating a dish that is both simple and satisfying.

Typical Mealtimes: Usually served for lunch or dinner, often on special occasions such as weddings and national celebrations.

Traditions & Rituals: Seswaa is a dish of honor. It's prepared by men at large gatherings, symbolizing unity and hospitality.

Dining Tips & Etiquette:

- Use a spoon or your hands to eat when served with porridge.
- When dining in a home, wait for the eldest person to take the first bite.
- Complimenting the cook is always appreciated—say **"Go monate!"** (It's delicious!).

Morogo – Botswana's Nutritious Wild Spinach

Main Ingredients & Flavors: Wild leafy greens, onion, tomato, and a touch of salt. Some variations include **peanut butter** for extra richness.

Estimated Budget: 10–50 BWP ($1–$4) per serving.

Where to Find It (GPS Locations):

- **Botswana Craft, Gaborone** (GPS: -24.6575, 25.9082)
- **Bojanala Waterfront, Gaborone** (GPS: -24.6536, 25.9125)
- **Local street vendors and markets across Botswana**

Preparation: The greens are washed thoroughly, boiled, and lightly sautéed with onions and tomatoes. In some homes, they are ground into a paste with peanuts.

Taste Profile: Earthy and slightly bitter, balanced with the sweetness of onion and tomato. The peanut variation adds a creamy, nutty depth.

Typical Mealtimes: Served at lunch or dinner as a side dish, often paired with porridge or meat.

Traditions & Rituals: Morogo is considered a symbol of health and strength. Elders often encourage children to eat it for good eyesight.

Dining Tips & Etiquette:

- Eat it with a fork or mix it into porridge with your hands.
- If invited to a local meal, accept morogo—it's a sign of respect for traditional food.
- To compliment the cook, say **"Ke ratile morogo!"** (I like the morogo!).

Bogobe – The Staple Porridge

Main Ingredients & Flavors: Sorghum or maize meal, water. Often enjoyed plain or mixed with milk, sugar, or butter.

Estimated Budget: 10–40 BWP ($1–$3) per serving.

Where to Find It (GPS Locations):

- **Main Mall Market, Gaborone** (GPS: -24.6569, 25.9087)
- **Sedia Riverside Hotel, Maun** (GPS: -19.9825, 23.4183)
- **Home kitchens and traditional events across Botswana**

Preparation: The grain is ground into fine flour, slowly cooked with water to a thick, smooth consistency. Some variations include fermented porridge (**ting**), which has a tangy taste.

Taste Profile: Mild and creamy, absorbing the flavors of whatever it's paired with—meat, milk, or vegetables.

Typical Mealtimes: Eaten throughout the day—plain for breakfast, with meat for lunch, or as a comforting evening meal.

Traditions & Rituals: In many households, the first bowl of freshly made porridge is given to the elders as a sign of respect.

Dining Tips & Etiquette:

- If served in a communal bowl, use only your right hand to scoop.
- Stirring porridge in a clockwise motion is considered good luck.
- Say **"Bogobe bo monate!"** (The porridge is tasty!) to express gratitude.

Mopane Worms – A Crunchy Delicacy

Main Ingredients & Flavors: Dried mopane caterpillars, salt, chili, onion, tomato.

Estimated Budget: 20–80 BWP ($2–$6) per serving.

Where to Find It (GPS Locations):

- **Gaborone Main Market, Gaborone** (GPS: -24.6571, 25.9085)
- **Maun Market, Maun** (GPS: -19.9842, 23.4189)
- **Village food stalls across the country**

Preparation: The worms are cleaned, boiled, and either sun-dried for snacking or cooked with onion and tomato into a stew.

Taste Profile: Smoky, slightly nutty, and chewy when dried; tender and rich when stewed.

Typical Mealtimes: Eaten as a snack or side dish, especially in rural areas.

Traditions & Rituals: Mopane worms are a valuable source of protein and are often gathered by families in the wild during the rainy season.

Dining Tips & Etiquette:

- Don't be shy—trying them is a sign of respect for local culture.
- If unsure, start with the stewed version, which has a milder taste.
- Say **"Ke itumelela go leka dikgobe!"** (I'm happy to try mopane worms!).

Final Tips for Enjoying Botswana's Food Scene

- Meals are often eaten **family-style**, so expect to share.
- **Tipping** isn't mandatory but is appreciated in restaurants (5-10%).
- **Street food is safe**, but choose busy stalls for the freshest options.
- **Water is generally safe** in cities, but bottled water is recommended in rural areas.

Botswana's food is about more than just eating—it's about connection, history, and the warmth of the people who prepare it. Be open, try something new, and let the flavors tell their story.

Best Restaurants & Local Eateries

Botswana's dining scene is a flavorful mix of traditional cuisine and modern influences, offering everything from street-side stalls serving hearty local dishes to upscale restaurants presenting gourmet takes on regional flavors. Whether you're craving a slow-cooked beef stew, a perfectly grilled fillet of fish, or a refreshing sip of locally brewed beer, there's a place waiting to serve you. Here's where to go and what to eat when traveling through Botswana.

1. The Boma – Dinner & Drum Show

Address: Victoria Falls Safari Lodge, Stand 471 Squire Cummings Rd, Victoria Falls, Zimbabwe (Near Botswana Border)

GPS: -17.9243, 25.8416

For a lively evening filled with the flavors of Botswana and Southern Africa, The Boma is an experience worth having. The open-air setting, complete with traditional drumming and dance performances, makes for a festive atmosphere. Guests can enjoy everything from warthog steak to Botswana's staple, seswaa (slow-cooked shredded beef), alongside an array of game meats and vegetarian options. The dining experience includes an interactive element, where visitors are encouraged to try mopane worms, a local delicacy.

Estimated Price: $30–$50 per person

What to Eat & Drink:

- Seswaa with pap (maize porridge)
- Kudu, crocodile, or warthog steak
- Traditional sorghum beer or a bottle of South African wine

2. Sanitas Tea Garden

Address: Gaborone, Botswana, Next to the National Botanical Gardens
GPS: -24.6865, 25.9110

Set within a lush nursery, this peaceful café is a favorite for a relaxed breakfast or lunch in Gaborone. The menu features fresh, homemade meals, including hearty sandwiches, gourmet salads, and baked goods. The outdoor seating under shady trees provides a cool retreat from the midday heat.

Estimated Price: $10–$20 per person

What to Eat & Drink:

- Homemade quiche with a side salad
- Rooibos iced tea
- Freshly baked scones with jam and cream

3. The Beef Baron Grillhouse

Address: Grand Palm Hotel, Gaborone

GPS: -24.6326, 25.9238

For meat lovers, The Beef Baron is the place to be. This steakhouse is known for its high-quality cuts, expertly grilled to perfection. The restaurant sources its beef from local farms, ensuring fresh and tender meat. The elegant setting makes it ideal for a special night out.

Estimated Price: $25–$50 per person

What to Eat & Drink:

- Aged Botswana beef fillet
- Oxtail stew with samp

- A glass of South African Pinotage

4. Mokolodi Restaurant

Address: Mokolodi Nature Reserve, Gaborone

GPS: -24.7333, 25.7854

Nestled inside a wildlife reserve, Mokolodi Restaurant offers a dining experience surrounded by nature. The menu features a mix of traditional Botswana meals and international favorites, with an emphasis on fresh, locally sourced ingredients. It's an excellent spot to unwind after a game drive.

Estimated Price: $15–$30 per person

What to Eat & Drink:

- Slow-cooked goat stew
- Chakalaka (spicy vegetable relish) with grilled chicken
- Marula fruit liqueur

5. Bull & Bush Pub

Address: Gaborone, Botswana

GPS: -24.6281, 25.9219

A lively pub and grill offering hearty meals and a great selection of drinks, Bull & Bush is popular with locals and travelers alike. The outdoor beer garden is perfect for socializing, while the indoor space offers a warm, welcoming atmosphere.

Estimated Price: $10–$25 per person

What to Eat & Drink:

- Grilled T-bone steak
- Classic fish and chips
- Botswana-brewed St. Louis beer

6. Chutney Restaurant

Address: Plot 5624, Gaborone

GPS: -24.6540, 25.9112

For those craving Indian cuisine, Chutney Restaurant delivers flavorful curries, fragrant biryanis, and homemade naan bread. The menu caters to both vegetarians and meat lovers, and the portions are generous.

Estimated Price: $10–$20 per person

What to Eat & Drink:

- Butter chicken with garlic naan
- Lentil dal with basmati rice
- Mango lassi

7. Tandurei Indian Restaurant

Address: Gaborone, Botswana

GPS: -24.6548, 25.9115

Another excellent spot for Indian food, Tandurei is known for its tandoori dishes and rich curries. The ambiance is cozy, making it a great choice for an intimate dinner.

Estimated Price: $15–$30 per person

What to Eat & Drink:

- Tandoori chicken
- Lamb rogan josh
- Sweet lassi

Bush Dinners & Dining Under the Stars

The air is warm, carrying the scent of acacia wood burning softly in the distance. Overhead, a sky untouched by city lights stretches endlessly, studded with stars that seem to flicker in time with the crackling fire. The sounds of the African night—distant lion roars, the rhythmic chirp of crickets, and the occasional call of a nightjar—set the backdrop for a dining experience unlike any other.

Bush dinners in Botswana are not just about the food; they are about the setting, the atmosphere, and the sense of connection to the land. Whether you find yourself seated at a long, lantern-lit table beneath ancient baobabs or on the banks of the Okavango Delta with hippos grunting in the distance, each meal tells a story of the wilderness.

What to Expect

The Setting

Bush dinners take place in remote, breathtaking locations—deep in the heart of game reserves, along riverbanks, or in open plains where the horizon seems endless. Some are arranged as an extension of a safari, where guests arrive after an evening game drive to find tables set up under the stars. Others are more intimate affairs, with private setups for honeymooners or small groups.

Lanterns and flickering firelight set a warm glow, while carefully placed seating blends seamlessly into the environment. Some lodges take it a step further, arranging traditional reed enclosures for a more authentic feel, with woven mats and low wooden tables adding to the charm.

The Cuisine

Meals at a bush dinner are thoughtfully prepared, combining local ingredients with international flavors. Expect meats like kudu, impala, and beef, often grilled over an open flame, paired with fresh vegetables and hearty side dishes. Traditional Botswana dishes such as **seswaa** (slow-cooked, shredded beef) and **morogo** (wild spinach) make frequent appearances, bringing a touch of local flavor to the table.

For those with a taste for something adventurous, some chefs incorporate seasonal game meats, prepared with skill and respect for the region's culinary heritage. And then there are the fresh-baked breads, chutneys, and homemade desserts—often featuring marula fruit or baobab-infused flavors—that round out the experience.

The Atmosphere

Dining under the stars in Botswana is about more than just good food. It is a chance to step away from the modern world and into something timeless. The sky, undisturbed by artificial light, becomes a spectacle in itself. Guides often bring along telescopes or share stories of how the San people read the constellations for guidance.

Some dinners are accompanied by live music, with local musicians playing traditional instruments like the **segaba**, a single-stringed fiddle, or the deep, rhythmic beats of a marimba. Others are more tranquil, with only the sounds of the wild filling the silence between conversations.

Special Occasions & Private Dinners

Many lodges and safari camps offer private bush dinners for honeymooners, anniversaries, or special celebrations. These can include personal chefs, candlelit tables set apart from the main group, and menus tailored to individual preferences.

For those traveling with family or in a group, communal dinners around a firepit create an inviting space where stories flow as freely as the wine. Some camps even host traditional **boma** nights, where guests dine in a circular enclosure, often accompanied by local dancers sharing Botswana's vibrant cultural heritage.

Practical Information

When to Go

Bush dinners are available year-round, though the experience shifts with the seasons. The dry months (May to October) bring clear skies and cool evenings, perfect for fireside dining. During the wetter months (November to April), dinners are often set up under covered platforms or beneath large trees to shield from occasional showers, but the warm air and fresh scents of the season add their own charm.

What to Wear

Evenings in the bush can be cooler than expected, especially in winter, so it's wise to bring a light jacket or shawl. Comfortable, neutral-colored clothing helps blend into the environment, while closed-toe shoes are recommended in case you find yourself walking on uneven ground.

Booking & Availability

Most safari lodges and camps include bush dinners as part of their stay, though private setups often require advance booking. It's always good to check whether dietary restrictions can be accommodated—most places are happy to tailor meals for vegetarian, vegan, or allergy-conscious travelers.

A Night to Remember

A bush dinner in Botswana is more than just a meal—it is a moment in time, shared with the land and its creatures. The stars overhead, the fire's glow, the distant calls of the wild—it all lingers in memory long after the last plate has been cleared.

Street Food & Market Experiences

There's no better way to understand a place than through its food, and in Botswana, the streets and markets offer an authentic window into daily life. Stalls filled with sizzling meats, fresh produce, and time-honored recipes bring together flavors shaped by generations. Whether you're strolling through a bustling market in Gaborone or pausing at a roadside vendor in Maun, each bite tells a story of tradition, resourcefulness, and the deep connection between food and community.

Street Food: Bold Flavors from Open Flames

Botswana's street food is all about simplicity, quality ingredients, and bold flavors. Meat plays a starring role in many dishes, cooked over open fires that send plumes of smoky aroma through the air. Here's what to look for:

Seswaa: Botswana's Signature Dish

Slow-cooked beef or goat, pounded until tender and seasoned simply with salt, forms the base of **seswaa**. Served with **bogobe** (a thick sorghum porridge) or maize meal, it's a staple found everywhere—from roadside stalls to family celebrations. Vendors often ladle it onto plates straight from steaming pots, offering a no-fuss meal that's both hearty and deeply satisfying.

Magwinya: Botswana's Take on Fried Dough

Crispy on the outside, soft and airy within, **magwinya** (fat cakes) are the go-to street snack for a quick breakfast or midday bite. They're often paired with tea or eaten alongside polony, fried eggs, or even just a smear of peanut butter. Found in markets and at street corners, these golden bites are a must-try for any visitor.

Matanga (Roasted Mopane Worms)

For those feeling adventurous, **matanga** (mopane worms) provide a protein-rich snack packed with flavor. These caterpillars of the mopane moth are either sun-dried or cooked with tomatoes, onions, and a hint of chili. Crunchy when dried and slightly chewy when stewed, they're a favorite for their rich, umami-like taste.

BBQ & Braai Stalls: Grilled Meats on the Go

Fire-grilled meats are a staple, with vendors setting up braai (barbecue) stands along busy streets and market areas. **Beef, chicken, and goat skewers**, often marinated in simple spices, are grilled over open coals, served hot off the fire with fresh salads and **pap** (maize porridge).

Market Experiences: Colors, Aromas, and Lively Bargaining

Botswana's markets are more than just places to shop—they are the heart of the community, where locals gather to buy fresh produce, handmade crafts, and everyday essentials. Whether you're looking for traditional ingredients or a casual meal, markets are the perfect place to wander, watch, and taste.

Gaborone's Main Mall & Station Market

In the capital city, the **Main Mall Market** and nearby **Station Market** are hubs of activity. Stalls overflow with fresh fruits, vegetables, grains, and street food favorites. Vendors sell everything from roasted groundnuts and dried fruits to spices and homemade relishes. It's also a great place to find traditional biltong (cured, spiced meat) and **serobe**, a dish made from slow-cooked offal, often enjoyed by those who appreciate rich, deep flavors.

Maun's Market Scene

As the gateway to the Okavango Delta, Maun's markets reflect the rhythms of both town life and rural communities. Farmers from surrounding villages bring seasonal goods—think wild honey, marula nuts, and locally grown produce—while artisans sell handwoven baskets and beadwork. Food stalls here serve up fresh fish from the nearby rivers, along with stews and grilled meats cooked over open flames.

Francistown's Fresh Produce Markets

Francistown, one of Botswana's oldest towns, has vibrant markets filled with fresh produce, grains, and meats. Local favorites include **lekuka**, a fermented milk drink, and homemade ginger beer, often sold in repurposed glass bottles.

Tips for Enjoying Street Food & Markets

- **Go Early for Fresh Finds** – Morning is the best time to explore markets, as vendors set up fresh produce and prepare daily specials.

- **Bring Small Bills & Coins** – Many vendors deal in cash, and exact change makes transactions easier.

- **Try Local Specialties** – If unsure what to eat, ask vendors what's popular that day. They're usually happy to share recommendations.

- **Be Open to New Tastes** – Some flavors and textures may be unfamiliar, but that's part of the experience. Mopane worms, for instance, may seem unusual at first but are a protein-rich delicacy enjoyed across the country.

- **Watch for the Busiest Stalls** – A line of locals is usually a sign of fresh and well-prepared food.

Chapter 10: Adventure Itineraries: The Perfect Trips for Every Traveler

Botswana's landscapes set the stage for journeys filled with wildlife encounters, open skies, and unforgettable moments. Whether you have a weekend or two weeks, these itineraries take you through the Okavango Delta's waterways, the Kalahari's vast deserts, and cultural gems along the way—tailored for first-time visitors and seasoned travelers alike.

7-Day Classic Botswana Safari Itinerary

Botswana is a land where wildlife still reigns, where elephants roam free, and where the Okavango Delta floods life into an untouched wilderness. A safari here isn't just a trip—it's an experience that stays with you long after you've left. This seven-day journey through some of Botswana's most incredible landscapes is designed to capture the magic of the bush, balancing adventure with comfort.

Each day includes morning, afternoon, and evening activities, ensuring that every moment counts. Expect thrilling game drives, peaceful mokoro (canoe) excursions, and nights under vast African skies. An estimated budget is also included to help with planning.

Estimated Budget Overview (Per Person)

- **Mid-range safari:** $4,500 – $6,500
- **Luxury safari:** $8,000 – $15,000

- **Budget safari (self-drive & camping):** $2,500 – $4,000 Prices vary depending on accommodations, park fees, and activities.

Day 1: Arrival in Maun – Gateway to the Wilderness

Morning

- Arrive at **Maun International Airport (MUB)**
- Meet your safari guide or transfer to your lodge
- Breakfast at **The Duck Café**—a relaxing spot along the Thamalakane River

Afternoon

- Explore Maun: Visit the Nhabe Museum or take a short cultural tour
- Final gear check for the safari ahead

Evening

- Sunset cruise on the Thamalakane River with drinks and snacks
- Overnight at **Thamalakane River Lodge** ($250–$400 per night) or **Maun Backpackers** ($50–$100 per night for budget travelers)

Day 2: Okavango Delta – Into the Wild

Morning

- Early flight or boat transfer into the Okavango Delta
- Check-in at a delta lodge or mobile safari camp
- Guided walking safari—perfect for tracking wildlife on foot

Afternoon

- Traditional mokoro (dugout canoe) safari through the winding waterways
- Picnic lunch in the bush, surrounded by the sounds of the delta

Evening

- Sunset game drive in search of lions, leopards, and wild dogs
- Traditional dinner by the fire, storytelling from guides
- Overnight at **Xugana Island Lodge ($700–$1,200 per night) or Moremi Crossing ($450–$700 per night)**

Day 3: Moremi Game Reserve – Predators & Prey

Morning

- Dawn game drive—this is when predators are most active
- Breakfast at camp, then a bush walk to track smaller creatures

Afternoon

- Relax at the lodge or take an optional fishing trip
- Midday game drive to spot elephants, giraffes, and zebra

Evening

- Sundowners on a scenic riverbank
- Night drive with a spotlight to search for nocturnal wildlife
- Overnight at **Camp Xakanaxa ($600–$1,000 per night) or Third Bridge Camp ($150–$400 per night for budget travelers)**

Day 4: Khwai Concession – Where the Action Is

Morning

- Leisurely boat cruise to Khwai or drive from Moremi
- Check into an intimate tented camp
- Brunch overlooking the floodplains

Afternoon

- Off-road game drive in private concession areas
- Watch hippos, buffalo, and rare antelope at waterholes

Evening

- Night safari—look for leopards, civets, and bush babies
- Traditional dinner at camp
- Overnight at **Khwai River Lodge ($800–$1,500 per night) or Magotho Campsite ($50–$150 per night for camping)**

Day 5: Savuti – The Land of Giants

Morning

- Drive or fly to Savuti in **Chobe National Park**
- Game drive en route, stopping for wildlife sightings
- Breakfast at camp with views of the dry Savuti Channel

Afternoon

- Search for the famous Savuti lion prides and large elephant herds
- Visit ancient San Bushman rock paintings

Evening

- Bush dinner with local dishes
- Campfire storytelling and stargazing
- Overnight at **Savute Safari Lodge ($750–$1,300 per night) or Savuti Campsite ($100–$300 per night)**

Day 6: Chobe National Park – The Elephant Kingdom

Morning

- Transfer to Chobe's riverfront
- Check-in at a riverside lodge or mobile safari camp
- Boat cruise along the Chobe River—elephants crossing the water is a sight to remember

Afternoon

- Leisure time at the lodge, followed by an afternoon game drive
- Spotting herds of buffalo, giraffes, and predators waiting for nightfall

Evening

- Sunset river cruise with drinks and snacks
- Farewell dinner under the stars
- Overnight at **Chobe Game Lodge ($800–$1,500 per night) or Chobe Safari Lodge ($400–$700 per night)**

Day 7: Kasane & Departure

Morning

- Final sunrise safari or relaxing morning by the river
- Breakfast before transferring to Kasane Airport for departure

Optional Afternoon Extension

- Visit **Victoria Falls (1-hour drive from Kasane)** for a breathtaking end to your journey
- Helicopter ride over the falls ($150–$250 per person)
- Overnight in Victoria Falls if extending the trip

Final Notes on Budget & Planning

- **Park fees:** $30–$50 per day
- **Game drives & activities:** Included in most lodges, otherwise $50–$150 per activity
- **Domestic flights (Maun to Delta, Delta to Savuti, etc.):** $300–$600 per flight
- **Tipping guides & staff:** $10–$20 per day
- **Travel insurance recommended**

10-Day Ultimate Adventure: From Okavango to the Kalahari

Botswana offers an unmatched blend of raw wilderness, thriving wildlife, and breathtaking landscapes. This 10-day adventure takes you from the Okavango Delta's winding waterways to the vast, open stretches of the Kalahari Desert. Each day is packed with activities that let you connect with nature, experience local culture, and witness some of the most extraordinary wildlife spectacles on Earth.

Day 1: Arrival in Maun – Gateway to the Okavango Delta

Morning:

- Arrive in Maun, the hub for most safaris into the Delta.
- Check in at a comfortable lodge like Thamalakane River Lodge ($150–$250 per night).
- Enjoy a riverside breakfast before preparing for the adventure ahead.

Afternoon:

- Take a scenic flight over the Okavango Delta ($120–$180 per person). The aerial view of the winding channels, animal herds, and lush islands is mesmerizing.
- Visit the Nhabe Museum to learn about the local culture and history ($5 entry fee).

Evening:

- Dine at The Duck, a local favorite serving fresh, well-prepared meals ($15–$25 per meal).
- Relax by the river with a sundowner, preparing for the wild ahead.

Day 2: Okavango Delta – Mokoro Safari & Walking Tour

Morning:

- Depart for the Okavango Delta by boat or light aircraft transfer ($100–$150 per person).
- Hop into a traditional mokoro (dugout canoe) and glide through the channels, spotting elephants, hippos, and vibrant birdlife.

Afternoon:

- Set up at a luxury tented camp such as Kanana or Moremi Crossing ($300–$600 per night).
- Join a guided walking safari led by local trackers, where you can see wildlife up close.

Evening:

- Traditional dinner under the stars, featuring local dishes like seswaa (pounded meat) and pap ($20–$40 per meal).
- Nighttime storytelling with your guides around the campfire.

Day 3: Moremi Game Reserve – Big Game Safari

Morning:

- Early game drive in Moremi Game Reserve, one of Botswana's richest wildlife areas.
- Watch lions, leopards, and wild dogs hunt as the sun rises.

Afternoon:

- Picnic lunch in the bush, followed by more wildlife viewing.
- Optional boat safari along the river ($50–$80 per person).

Evening:
- Sundowners at the lodge, then a candlelit bush dinner.
- Rest well before another day of adventure.

Day 4: Transfer to Savuti – Predator Country

Morning:
- Transfer to Savuti, known for its high concentration of big cats ($200–$400 per person for charter flights or guided drive).
- Check into a safari lodge like Savute Safari Lodge ($450–$900 per night).

Afternoon:
- Game drive along the Savuti Channel, famous for its dramatic wildlife interactions.
- Visit ancient San Bushmen rock paintings.

Evening:
- Dinner at the lodge, then a night drive for a chance to see nocturnal wildlife like leopards and hyenas.

Day 5: Chobe National Park – The Elephant Capital

Morning:
- Early transfer to Chobe National Park ($150–$250 per person).
- Game drive in the Serondela area, home to the world's largest elephant population.

Afternoon:

- River cruise on the Chobe River ($50–$80 per person), a prime opportunity to see elephants, buffalo, and crocodiles.

Evening:

- Sunset dinner on a boat, enjoying local cuisine while hippos grunt nearby.
- Stay overnight at Chobe Game Lodge ($400–$700 per night).

Day 6: Kasane & Local Village Visit

Morning:

- Leisurely breakfast at the lodge, followed by a cultural visit to a local village ($20 donation recommended).

Afternoon:

- Take a short drive to Kasane Hot Springs for a relaxing soak.

Evening:

- Enjoy dinner at The Old House, a cozy riverside restaurant ($20–$40 per meal).

Day 7: Makgadikgadi Pans – The Endless Salt Flats

Morning:

- Transfer to Makgadikgadi Pans ($250–$500 per person, includes guided safari experience).
- Visit Kubu Island, a sacred granite outcrop in the salt flats.

Afternoon:

- Quad biking across the vast, empty salt pan.

Evening:

- Sleep under the open sky on a bedroll, an unforgettable experience.

Day 8: Central Kalahari – The Land of Giants

Morning:

- Travel to Central Kalahari Game Reserve ($300–$600 per person for guided transfer).
- Game drive to spot black-maned lions and cheetahs.

Afternoon:

- Visit a San Bushmen village to learn about traditional survival skills.

Evening:

- Enjoy a bush dinner at a lodge like Deception Valley Lodge ($350–$700 per night).

Day 9: Exploring the Kalahari

Morning:

- Morning nature walk with San guides.

Afternoon:

- Relax at the lodge or take another game drive.

Evening:

- Final sundowner in the wild, reflecting on the adventure.

Day 10: Return to Maun & Departure

Morning:

- Early morning transfer back to Maun ($150–$300 per person).
- Visit a local craft market for souvenirs.

Afternoon:

- Flight home or onward journey.

Estimated Total Budget (Per Person):

- Flights (international & domestic): $1,500–$3,000
- Accommodation (mix of lodges & camping): $3,000–$7,000
- Safaris, activities & park fees: $2,000–$5,000
- Meals & drinks: $500–$1,500
- Miscellaneous (tips, souvenirs, insurance): $500–$1,000 **Total Estimated Cost: $7,500–$17,500**

14-Day Wildlife & Cultural Immersion Trip

Day 1: Arrival in Maun – Gateway to the Okavango Delta

- **Morning:** Arrive in Maun, the safari hub of Botswana. Transfer to your lodge or guesthouse. Rest and freshen up.

- **Afternoon:** Take a scenic flight over the Okavango Delta ($120–$250 per person). The bird's-eye view of winding waterways and wildlife below is breathtaking.
- **Evening:** Enjoy a welcome dinner at a riverside restaurant ($15–$30 per meal) while watching the sunset over the Thamalakane River.

Estimated Budget: $200–$350 (including accommodation, meals, and activities)

Day 2: Mokoro Excursion & Bush Walk in the Okavango Delta

- **Morning:** Depart for a mokoro (traditional canoe) excursion deep into the delta ($80–$150 per person). Glide through the serene waters while spotting hippos, crocodiles, and colorful birds.
- **Afternoon:** Break for a bush lunch prepared by local guides, then enjoy a guided nature walk on one of the delta's islands.
- **Evening:** Return to your lodge for a fireside dinner with traditional storytelling.

Estimated Budget: $150–$300

Day 3: Moremi Game Reserve – Big Five Safari Begins

- **Morning:** Drive or take a charter flight ($200–$350) to Moremi Game Reserve, one of Africa's prime wildlife viewing spots.
- **Afternoon:** Set out on your first game drive ($100–$200 per person), searching for elephants, lions, leopards, and rare wild dogs.
- **Evening:** Camp in the wilderness or stay in a lodge ($150–$500 per night), listening to the sounds of nature as the night unfolds.

Estimated Budget: $300–$700

Day 4: Full-Day Safari in Moremi

- **Morning:** Sunrise game drive with a packed breakfast, tracking predators in their prime hunting hours.
- **Afternoon:** Visit the Xakanaxa Lagoon, a hotspot for birdwatching and hippo sightings.
- **Evening:** Enjoy a candlelit dinner at camp, sharing stories with fellow travelers.

Estimated Budget: $250–$600

Day 5: Transfer to Khwai Community Area – Cultural Experience & Wildlife Viewing

- **Morning:** Drive to Khwai ($50–$100 for a transfer) and settle into a community-run camp.
- **Afternoon:** Explore Khwai's wildlife-rich floodplains with a local guide.
- **Evening:** Visit a nearby village, interact with locals, and enjoy a cultural dance performance.

Estimated Budget: $200–$400

Day 6: Boat Safari & Night Drive in Khwai

- **Morning:** Enjoy a boat safari ($60–$150) along the Khwai River.
- **Afternoon:** Rest at camp or join an optional guided walk.

- **Evening:** Go on a night safari ($80–$200) to spot elusive nocturnal predators.

Estimated Budget: $250–$500

Day 7: Transfer to Savuti – Predator Country

- **Morning:** Drive to Savuti in Chobe National Park ($50–$150 for transfer).
- **Afternoon:** Game drive through Savuti's lion-dominated landscapes.
- **Evening:** Relax at camp under the star-studded sky.

Estimated Budget: $250–$600

Day 8: Exploring Savuti – Land of Giants

- **Morning:** Full-day safari in Savuti ($100–$250), known for its large elephant herds and lion-buffalo interactions.
- **Afternoon:** Visit ancient San rock paintings.
- **Evening:** Sunset drinks at a remote lookout point.

Estimated Budget: $250–$600

Day 9: Chobe National Park – The Land of Elephants

- **Morning:** Drive to Chobe Riverfront ($100–$250 for transfer).
- **Afternoon:** Boat safari on the Chobe River ($50–$150), watching herds of elephants bathing.
- **Evening:** Sunset photography session.

Estimated Budget: $200–$500

Day 10: Victoria Falls Excursion (Optional)

- **Morning:** Cross into Zimbabwe/Zambia ($50 visa fee) to witness Victoria Falls ($30 entry fee).
- **Afternoon:** Take a helicopter ride or a white-water rafting trip ($150–$300 per person).
- **Evening:** Return to Kasane, Botswana, for a relaxed dinner.

Estimated Budget: $300–$700

Day 11: Nata Bird Sanctuary – Flamingo Paradise

- **Morning:** Drive to Nata ($50–$150 for transfer).
- **Afternoon:** Visit the Makgadikgadi Salt Pans and Nata Bird Sanctuary.
- **Evening:** Stay in a safari lodge or campsite near the pans.

Estimated Budget: $150–$400

Day 12: Makgadikgadi Pans – Sleeping Under the Stars

- **Morning:** Explore the vast salt flats, meeting meerkats and learning about the pans' history.
- **Afternoon:** Quad biking ($100–$200 per person) across the pans.
- **Evening:** Sleep under the open sky with a local guide.

Estimated Budget: $250–$500

Day 13: Return to Maun – Relaxation & Shopping

- **Morning:** Drive back to Maun.
- **Afternoon:** Visit Nhabe Museum and local craft markets.
- **Evening:** Farewell dinner at a lodge.

Estimated Budget: $150–$400

Day 14: Departure

- **Morning:** Leisure time before transferring to the airport ($10–$50 for transport).

Estimated Budget: $50–$150

Estimated Total Budget for 14 Days: $4,000–$12,000 (varies based on lodging, activities, and transport choices).

Weekend Getaways & Short Trips for Time-Conscious Travelers

Even with just a few days to spare, Botswana delivers remarkable experiences that blend adventure, wildlife, and cultural depth. Whether it's an escape into the Okavango Delta, a quick safari in Chobe National Park, or a cultural retreat in Gaborone, these getaways maximize every moment without feeling rushed.

Okavango Delta: A Water Wonderland in Just a Weekend

Why Go

The Okavango Delta is a marvel of nature, a vast inland river system that transforms the landscape into a lush haven teeming with wildlife. Even a short visit offers a taste of this tranquil yet thriving ecosystem.

What to Do

- **Mokoro Canoe Safari:** Glide through reed-lined channels in a traditional dugout canoe, guided by skilled polers who know these waters intimately.
- **Walking Safari:** Instead of viewing animals from a vehicle, step onto the land and see elephants, antelopes, and exotic birds up close.
- **Scenic Flights:** A quick way to appreciate the Delta's maze of waterways, floodplains, and islands from above.

Where to Stay

- **Luxury:** Xugana Island Lodge – A secluded retreat with open-air chalets overlooking the water.
- **Mid-Range:** Moremi Crossing – A tented camp that balances comfort with the feel of the wild.
- **Budget:** Camping at Third Bridge – Ideal for those who prefer a raw, close-to-nature experience.

Chobe National Park: A Wildlife Spectacle in 48 Hours

Why Go

Chobe is renowned for its incredible elephant population, but that's just the beginning. Lions, buffalo, hippos, and a staggering variety of birdlife make every game drive or boat safari unforgettable.

What to Do

- **Boat Safari on the Chobe River:** Watch elephants wade through the water and hippos laze in the shallows, all while enjoying a tranquil cruise.

- **Game Drives:** Whether at dawn or dusk, these drives offer close encounters with predators and herbivores alike.

- **Sunset at the Riverbanks:** The sight of the sun dipping below the horizon, silhouetting animals against the sky, is something you won't forget.

Where to Stay

- **Luxury:** Chobe Game Lodge – A refined riverside stay offering excellent views and service.

- **Mid-Range:** Chobe Safari Lodge – Close to the park entrance, with comfortable chalets and a great restaurant.

- **Budget:** Thebe River Safaris – A laid-back spot with affordable rooms and camping options.

Gaborone: Culture, History, and Relaxation in the Capital

Why Go

Not every trip needs to be about the wild. Botswana's capital provides a mix of history, local markets, and laid-back dining experiences, perfect for a short city break.

What to Do

- **Visit the National Museum and Art Gallery:** Gain insight into Botswana's heritage through exhibits on traditional crafts, history, and contemporary art.

- **Hike Kgale Hill:** A short climb rewards you with panoramic views of the city and surrounding countryside.
- **Mokolodi Nature Reserve:** Just outside the city, this reserve offers game drives and the chance to interact with rescued animals.

Where to Stay

- **Luxury:** The Grand Palm Hotel – A stylish stay with a casino and spa.
- **Mid-Range:** Cresta Lodge – Conveniently located with modern comforts.
- **Budget:** Apartments or guesthouses near the city center provide affordable, cozy stays.

Makgadikgadi Pans: An Otherworldly Escape in Two Days

Why Go

These salt pans stretch endlessly, creating an atmosphere unlike anywhere else. A short visit offers the chance to witness wildlife, surreal landscapes, and ancient baobabs.

What to Do

- **Quad Biking on the Pans:** A thrilling way to explore the vast expanse.
- **Meet the Meerkats:** Some colonies are habituated to humans, allowing for close encounters.
- **Baobab Exploration:** The towering trees at Baines' Baobabs have stood for centuries, making for a humbling sight.

Where to Stay

- **Luxury:** Jack's Camp – A refined, tented camp that transports guests to another era.

- **Mid-Range:** Planet Baobab – A quirky and comfortable lodge with a fantastic atmosphere.

- **Budget:** Wild camping under the stars offers an experience unlike any other

Conclusion: Making the Most of Your Botswana Adventure

Botswana leaves a lasting impression, whether you've wandered through its untamed wilderness, cruised along the Okavango Delta, or stood in awe of elephants at Chobe. As your journey comes to an end, a few final thoughts can help you head home with unforgettable memories. A well-packed bag and a few insider tips can make all the difference, whether you're planning a return trip or sharing stories with friends. From must-have essentials to advice only seasoned travelers know, this section will ensure you feel prepared, inspired, and ready for your next adventure—because Botswana always has more to offer.

Final Travel Tips & Insider Recommendations

Botswana has a way of pulling you in—its vast landscapes, roaming wildlife, and warm-hearted people leave an imprint that lasts well beyond your journey. Before you pack up your memories and head home, a few final tips will help you wrap up your adventure smoothly and maybe even start planning your return.

1. Timing Your Travels Right

Botswana's seasons play a big role in shaping your experience. The dry months (May to October) bring cooler temperatures and prime wildlife viewing as animals gather around dwindling water sources. The wetter months (November to April) transform the land, bringing lush greenery, flowing rivers, and an influx of migratory birds. If you prefer quieter camps and a softer side of the wilderness, the shoulder seasons—April to May and late October—strike a balance between the two.

2. Handling Money & Payments

The official currency, the Botswana Pula (BWP), is widely accepted, but cash is still important, especially in remote areas. While credit cards work in lodges and bigger towns, national parks and small villages often operate on cash. ATMs are available in cities like Maun, Gaborone, and Kasane, but don't count on them being reliable in rural areas. Always keep some smaller bills for tips, markets, and roadside stops.

3. Tipping Etiquette

Tipping isn't mandatory but is appreciated. Guides, trackers, and camp staff often rely on tips as part of their income. A good rule of thumb is:

- **Safari Guides**: $10–$20 per person per day
- **Trackers**: $5–$10 per person per day
- **Camp Staff**: A collective tip of around $5–$10 per day, given at the end of your stay Always hand tips directly to individuals rather than leaving them in a general tip box unless the lodge has specific guidelines.

4. Packing Smart for the Journey

A safari in Botswana doesn't call for fancy outfits, but it does require smart packing. Keep clothing lightweight, neutral-colored, and breathable. Long sleeves and pants protect against the sun and insects. A good hat, sunglasses, and sturdy walking shoes are non-negotiable. Pack a swimsuit for dips in lodge pools and a warm layer for chilly early mornings.

Essentials to Have on Hand:

- High-SPF sunscreen and insect repellent
- A refillable water bottle (many lodges offer filtered water)
- A good pair of binoculars—essential for game drives

- A flashlight or headlamp for navigating camp paths at night
- Extra camera batteries and memory cards—you'll take more photos than you expect

5. Respecting Local Customs & Wildlife

Botswana's people are welcoming, and showing a little respect goes a long way. A handshake is the common greeting, and taking time to exchange pleasantries before diving into conversation is appreciated. When visiting villages, ask permission before taking photos.

Out in the bush, patience and silence are rewarded. Don't pressure guides to get too close to animals, and never attempt to feed or touch wildlife. At camps, follow staff instructions—whether it's walking with a guide after dark or keeping food out of your tent to avoid uninvited visitors.

6. Staying Safe & Healthy

- **Malaria Precautions:** Northern Botswana, including the Okavango Delta and Chobe, is a malaria zone. Take antimalarial medication and use repellent, especially in the wet season.
- **Water Safety:** Tap water in cities is generally safe, but stick to filtered or bottled water in the bush.
- **Emergency Contacts:** Keep the details of your lodge, guide, and local embassy saved on your phone or written down in case of poor signal.

7. Souvenirs & Responsible Shopping

Botswana offers beautiful handmade crafts, from woven baskets to carved wooden animals and intricate beadwork. Buy directly from artisans or ethical shops that support local communities. Avoid products made from animal parts—elephant hair bracelets and carved ivory may be sold illegally, and taking them across borders can land you in trouble.

8. Making the Most of Your Last Days

If your safari ends in Maun or Kasane, spend a little time soaking in the local culture. Maun has a few relaxed riverside lodges perfect for unwinding, while Kasane offers sunset boat cruises along the Chobe River. If you're heading through Gaborone, stop by the craft markets or enjoy one final taste of Botswana's rich flavors—seswaa (slow-cooked beef) and fresh river bream are worth trying before you leave.

Botswana has a way of staying with you long after your footprints fade from its dusty roads. Whether this was your first visit or one of many, the landscapes, wildlife, and people leave stories to carry home. And who knows? Maybe next time, the elephants will remember you, too.

Packing Guide & Essentials Checklist

Packing for Botswana isn't just about throwing a few things in a bag—it's about preparing for the rhythm of the land, the shifting temperatures, and the unpredictable moments that make a trip unforgettable. Whether you're heading into the Okavango Delta, tracking wildlife in Chobe, or exploring the vast Makgadikgadi Pans, what you bring can make all the difference. Here's what you need to know before zipping up that suitcase.

1. The Right Bag for the Journey

If you're flying into a remote safari camp, weight limits are strict—usually 15–20 kg (33–44 lbs), including carry-on. Soft duffel bags work better than hard-shell suitcases since they fit easily into small aircraft cargo holds. Even if you're traveling by road, packing light makes moving between camps much easier.

2. Clothing: Function Over Fashion

Forget bright colors and bulky outfits. The key is comfort, breathability, and blending into the environment.

- **Shirts & Tops:** Neutral tones like khaki, beige, and olive help you stay cool and avoid attracting insects. Pack a mix of long-sleeve and short-sleeve shirts—lightweight fabrics protect against the sun while keeping you cool.

- **Pants & Shorts:** Convertible pants (the kind that zip off into shorts) are practical for shifting temperatures.

- **Outerwear:** Early mornings and evenings can be cold, even in summer. A fleece or lightweight jacket is essential, especially in winter (May–August).

- **Shoes:** Comfortable, closed-toe shoes are a must for walking safaris. If you'll be staying mostly in lodges, sturdy sandals or slip-on shoes will do for game drives and camp settings.

- **Hats & Accessories:** A wide-brimmed hat with a chin strap (to keep it from flying off on a bumpy ride) is far better than a baseball cap for sun protection. A lightweight scarf or buff helps with dust and wind.

Laundry Tip: Most lodges offer laundry services, so you don't need to overpack. Just be mindful that some camps wash clothes by hand and don't handle undergarments—you might need to wash those yourself.

3. Safari Essentials

Certain items will make your time in the bush far more enjoyable:

- **Binoculars:** Even if your guide has a pair, having your own lets you appreciate the finer details—whether it's a leopard lounging in a distant tree or a kingfisher diving into the water. A 8x42 or 10x42 magnification works well.

- **Camera Gear:** A DSLR or mirrorless camera with a zoom lens (200mm or more) is ideal for wildlife photography. If using a smartphone, bring a portable charger—safaris can last hours, and outlets aren't always available.

- **Headlamp/Flashlight:** Camps can be dimly lit, and nighttime walks between tents are safer with your own light.

- **Refillable Water Bottle:** Botswana is serious about conservation, and single-use plastics are discouraged. Many lodges provide filtered water—bring a bottle to refill throughout your trip.

- **Small Daypack:** Handy for carrying sunscreen, a camera, and a light jacket on game drives or boat excursions.

4. Health & Safety Must-Haves

- **Sunscreen & Lip Balm:** The African sun is unforgiving. High-SPF sunscreen and SPF lip balm are non-negotiable.

- **Insect Repellent:** A strong repellent with DEET or picaridin keeps mosquitoes and other biting insects at bay.

- **First-Aid Kit:** Camps have medical supplies, but it's good to carry basics—band-aids, antiseptic wipes, pain relievers, and any prescription medication you need.

- **Malaria Medication:** Northern Botswana is a malaria-risk zone. Speak with your doctor about preventive medication before traveling.

- **Electrolyte Sachets:** If you're spending long hours in the heat, staying hydrated is key. Electrolyte packets help replenish lost minerals.

5. Electronics & Adapters

Botswana uses Type D and Type M plugs (the same as South Africa). Most lodges run on solar power, and some may have limited charging hours. If you're bringing multiple devices, a power bank or solar charger will keep your gadgets running.

- **Universal Adapter:** If you're coming from outside Africa, this is essential.

- **Extra Memory Cards & Batteries:** You'll take more photos than expected, and charging options might be limited in remote camps.

- **Offline Maps & Apps:** Google Maps, Maps.me, or a GPS app can help if you're self-driving. Download maps before arriving—some areas have weak or no signal.

6. Travel Documents & Money

- **Passport & Visas:** Ensure your passport is valid for at least six months beyond your travel dates and has enough blank pages for entry stamps. Some nationalities require visas—check before departure.

- **Travel Insurance:** Unexpected delays, medical emergencies, or lost luggage can happen. A solid travel insurance plan gives peace of mind.

- **Cash & Cards:** While credit cards are accepted in major towns and lodges, cash is useful in smaller villages and for tips. The Botswana Pula (BWP) is the official currency, but US dollars are widely accepted at lodges.

7. Sustainable Packing Choices

Botswana's conservation efforts are among the strongest in Africa, and travelers can play a role in keeping the ecosystem intact.

- **Eco-Friendly Toiletries:** Many camps are in delicate environments where waste disposal is limited. Bring biodegradable soap, shampoo, and wet wipes.
- **No Single-Use Plastics:** Botswana has banned plastic bags, so use a reusable shopping bag for small purchases.
- **Respectful Shopping:** If buying souvenirs, choose handmade crafts from local artisans instead of mass-produced trinkets. Avoid anything made from animal products like ivory or tortoise shell—these are illegal and contribute to wildlife exploitation.